Follow Me!

Creating a Personal Brand with Twitter®

Sarah-Jayne Gratton
@grattongirl

WILEY

John Wiley & Sons, Inc.

For Dean, the love of my life. Together we've danced around trees, wished on the stars, and achieved immortality through our work together. Waking up beside you every morning is my greatest gift and my greatest honor.

For Charlotte. On the day you were born I was born again, too. You are by far my greatest achievement, and there's not a day that goes by when you don't make me proud. I love you so very much, my Charlie-girl.

To Irene, my honorary little sis. For your endless love, for your untiring support, and for being the blessing that you are and will continue to be every day of my life.

Follow Me!

Creating a Personal Brand with Twitter®

Follow Me! Creating a Personal Brand with Twitter®

Published by

John Wiley & Sons, Inc.

10475 Crosspoint Boulevard

Indianapolis, IN 46256

www.wiley.com

Copyright © 2012 by John Wiley & Sons, Inc.

Published simultaneously in Canada

ISBN: 978-1-118-33634-2

Manufactured in the United States of America

10 9 8 7 6 5 4 3 2 1

For general information on our other products and services or to obtain technical support, please contact our Customer Care Department within the U.S. at (877) 762-2974, outside the U.S. at (317) 572-3993 or fax (317) 572-4002.

Wiley also publishes its books in a variety of electronic formats and by print-on-demand. Some content that appears in standard print versions of this book may not be available in other formats. For more information about Wiley products, visit us at www.wiley.com.

Library of Congress Control Number: 2012937952

Colophon: This book was produced using the ITC Novarese typeface for the body text and Myriad Pro for the titles, caption text, and table text.

Acknowledgments

It takes a special team of people to turn a good idea into a great book, and I'm fortunate in having the support of such a special team, beginning with Aaron Black, who first presented the idea to me for a new Twitter book and gave me the honor of writing it.

I was then introduced to the incredibly talented Galen Gruman and Carol Person, who worked with my individual style to give the book its unique personality.

My special team extends out to Twitter itself and to those people who have shared their personal branding success stories and who continue to inspire me every day.

I'd like to also give my thanks to the developers of all the amazing Twitter tools I cover in Part Four of the book. Your dedication and talent have helped to make the Twitterverse an ever-evolving platform for personal branding success.

I'd like to extend special thanks to my wonderful husband, Dean Anthony Gratton, who provided several of the unique illustrations for the book.

And finally to you — the readers, followers, and fans — who have supported me throughout my social media journey. This book is for you.

Credits

Acquisitions Editor
Aaron Black

Editorial Director
Robyn Siesky

Business Manager
Amy Knies

Senior Marketing Manager
Sandy Smith

**Vice President and
Executive Group Publisher**
Richard Swadley

**Vice President and
Executive Publisher**
Barry Pruett

Editor
Carol Person, The Zango Group

Design and Layout
Galen Gruman, The Zango Group

Cover Designer
Michael E. Trent

Illustrations
Dean Anthony Gratton

**Copy Editing, Proofreading,
and Indexing**
The Zango Group

About the Author

 Sarah-Jayne Gratton is a celebrity author, television presenter, and former theater performer.

Sarah-Jayne is an influential social media persona (as @grattongirl), speaker, and writer, regularly featured in *Social Media Today* and other publications, including *In-Spires Lifestyle Magazine* and blogcritics.org.

Sarah-Jayne is the winner of a 2012 Shorty Award for the Best Twitter in Social Media and is one of Twitter's Top 75 Badass Women (#BA75). She is also listed as one of the top marketing book authors on Twitter in *Social Media Marketing Magazine*. Sarah-Jayne is the coproducer and host of online TV talent show TwittersGotTalent.TV, where contestants submit videos to the show and the Twitter community vote for their favorite act. TwittersGotTalent.TV was featured on the BBC's *Click* TV program.

Sarah-Jayne is listed in the Top 50 of *The Sunday Times* Social List.

She has a Bachelor of Arts in educational psychology and later received a doctorate in psychology.

You can contact Sarah-Jayne at assistant@sarahgratton.com and follow her on Twitter (@grattongirl) to enjoy her personal branding and social-media-related tweets. You can also read more about her work at www.sarahgratton.com.

Contents

Contents

Chapter 10: *Beyond Hashtags: Make Your Brand*   **113**
a Trending Topic

Part Three: **Twitter Branding Showcase Stories**   **123**

Chapter 11: *Empowering Health Care*   **127**

Chapter 12: *Changing the Job Market One Tweet at a Time*   **137**

Chapter 13: *Making Twitter Your Personal Brand Diary*   **143**

Chapter 14: *Social Media Entrepreneur at 17*   157

Chapter 15: *Meet the Twitter Ninja*   165

Chapter 16: *Tweeting around the World*   179

Chapter 17: *Putting Her Personal Brand in the Pink*   **189**

Chapter 18: *The 'Green' Giant of Twitter*   **199**

Chapter 19: *Twitter to the Power of Two*　　209

Part Four: **Twitter Toolkit: Supercharge Your Brand**　　219

Chapter 20: *Twitter Clients and Directories*　　223

"It's all become very personal indeed."

@grattongirl

The Rise of the Personal

It wasn't a sudden change. It didn't occur in a single earth-shattering moment of realization and there were certainly no anatomical transformations. But the change came: a gradual, distilling of that all-important bottom line with my own unique blend of self, resulting in a concoction so headily steeped in engagement that it became socially intoxicating.

And where did it all begin?

Like part of a dying herd of corporate cattle, I am one of many who escaped the heat of the traditional branding iron and transformed my business message into something personal — something me! The irony lies in the fact that this evolution came about as a result of a communications curfew to the tune of 140 characters. Suddenly, 'less' was the new 'more' and my personal polarities became fundamental to the way that my business communicated itself.

You see, what's happened is that Twitter has become far more than just the micro-blogging service initially intended. Even Jack Dorsey, its founder, couldn't have envisioned just how extraordinary the outcome of that initial team meeting over Mexican takeout in the park on that fateful afternoon would prove to be.

After all, Twitter has not only tuned into the way marketing has changed from a monolog to a two-way conversation-based system, it has been instrumental in its evolution. It's personalities, not pitches, that sell today. And it's not what you have to say to others that make your brand successful, it's what others have to say about you.

For smaller businesses and entrepreneurs, the shift has provided previously untold opportunities to compete with the big boys in their respective business arenas. And, as for the big boys themselves, it's been nothing short of a wake-up call. A time to put away the foghorn and start listening instead, as creativity rather than cash-flow takes the reins of brand adoption, while relationships and engagement become the new currency. It's all become very personal indeed.

In a 2011 Pivot survey done with the Hudson Group, it was discovered that 97 percent of businesses believed their brands would be "lifted" through social engagement, yet fewer than 40 percent had used the social sphere to determine what their evolved customer base actually wanted. Maybe they just weren't listening or maybe they were afraid to face facts, but the old-school methods and theories of marketing, the ones that many of the biggest brand names had cut their teeth on, are now archaic and rather sad. Call it the fear of the unknown, call it a security blanket. Whatever you call it, it's completely understandable. But understandable actions don't always move us forward; instead, they all too often keep us hovering in an abyss of uncertainty.

Immediacy and the Rise of the Social Consumer

In the brave new world of Twitter, the rise of the social consumer can no longer be ignored. I have personally cast asunder much of the traditional form of press in favor of trusted online resources to provide the news and information I crave each day and that, in turn, I share with my followers. My Twitter streams are carefully sectioned and categorized according to my wants and interests, and I no longer rely on third-party aggregated media sources to ascertain what's going on.

Moreover, a growing number of celebrities and high-profile personal brands have found that Twitter has handed them the keys to their old-media shackles, as more and more choose to use the platform to share the news and photos that keep them in the public eye through their daily tweets, without the need to rely solely on traditional press and paparazzi routes.

This new approach, however, can prove to be a double-edged sword — the phrase "once tweeted, never forgotten" springs to mind. The immediacy of Twitter means that once it's out there, *it's out there for good*, a fact that many have learned the hard way.

The role of the modern successful brand is an enabling one, one that listens and responds to the voice of its audience through engagement and empathy. If your brand provides value to the social consumer, it will become trusted and your social audience will over time become your *brand ambassadors*. It's a trust cycle (see Figure A-1) that, if adopted

FIGURE A-1

A trust cycle

correctly, will gain momentum and can lift the smallest personal brand to dizzying heights of success.

So what's happening? We're living in a relationship-based social ecosystem that has finally found its voice. Today's consumer has more power than ever and, no matter what size your brand may be, you need to accept and embrace that truth if you're to survive and thrive.

A Cautionary Tale

This brings me to damage limitation, something that I cover later in the book, but for now I want to focus on a single, incredibly profound case.

In January 2012, Minhee Cho (@mintymin) went into a Papa John's (@papajohns) pizza restaurant in New York for takeout. What she received that day was far more than just a pizza, however: It was a wake-up call into just how powerful her social voice was. Upon checking her receipt,

@mintymin
Minhee Cho
Follow @mintymin

Hey @PapaJohns just FYI my name isn't "lady chinky eyes"
http://t.co/RLdj2Eij

January 7, 2012 5:06 pm via Twitpic   Reply   Retweet   Favorite

Thank You For Choosing
Papa Johns
Restaurant # 3070
3477 Broadway
New York, NY 10031
(212) 368-7272
3989   01/06/2012   08:10pm
****
InStore Order

Name: lady chinky eyes
****
Restaurant Order #: 0113

FIGURE A-2

Minhee Cho's receipt from Papa John's, which set off a storm of protest via Twitter and showed the power of Twitter on brands

she noticed that they had printed her name as "lady chinky eyes" (as shown in Figure A-2).

At first, Minhee was upset by the clearly racist remark, but then she got angry and decided to share her experience with her Twitter followers by tweeting a photo of the receipt for all to see. It's worth mentioning here that @mintymin didn't have a huge following at that time — only a couple of thousand followers, in fact — but *that* fact is what makes this example even more powerful.

Within minutes, hundreds of outraged tweets began flooding in, each mentioning @papajohn, @mintymin, and the appalling customer service she had received. Her original tweet was retweeted over and over and was viewed by more than 250,000 people on Twitter within a week of it first being tweeted. That represented both a phenomenal consumer result and a phenomenal blow for Papa John's, which then spent weeks of work on damage limitation: investigating the outcry, firing the employee, and tweeting apologies. It was certainly a wake-up call for the company that now knew the full power of what Twitter can achieve in brand awareness — good and bad — and should be remembered as a cautionary tale for businesses that dare to take the power of the social consumer lightly.

Emotions and Relationship Rituals

The psychology of a personal brand begins and ends with emotions. It's what shapes our view of the world and how we experience our lives within it. The brands we grew up with form an emotional allegiance within us, and their logos act as triggers to moments and events that have shaped our lives. For me, the Heinz logo conjures up images of fireside suppers as a child: my grandmother humming in the kitchen as she happily stirred the pot of Heinz cream of tomato soup (my all-time favorite) while the wonderful aroma, combined with that of hot buttered toast, teased my taste buds and filled me with a deep sense of belonging and security.

My devotion to the brand has since been passed down to my daughter, who now finds immense comfort in her soup-and-toast supper rituals, where nothing other than the Heinz brand will do.

Another highly emotional brand is the phenomenon of Apple. Lovers of the brand are nothing short of fanatical about its products, content to queue for hours to purchase each latest offering the brand creates. Later in the book, I explore how Twitter has remodeled branding using relationship rituals that create an emotional bond between the person and the brand.

So what are these relationship rituals? They center on our need to feel connected to something other than ourselves, to feel that we are important and that our voices will be heard. Twitter came along at exactly the right time. Uncertainty was rife, economies were collapsing, and life felt a little more fragile. Suddenly, we found a way to reach out through the uncertainty, to share and to empathize, to bond and to build. Through Twitter, our online relationships became very personal as we entered a new frontier of communication.

This new frontier provides opportunities that were previously much harder, if not impossible, to obtain: the ability to listen to hundreds of conversations about our brands in real time. Consumers are online all day, every day, sharing and tweeting away about how they feel. Sentiment is oozing out of every tweet, and we should not fear it. Instead, we should embrace it as the new lifeblood of branding. The ability to listen and understand how consumers feel (whether good or bad), what is important to them, and what their expectations are provides huge opportunities for forming the emotional allegiances needed for enduring brand loyalty.

But having explained the emotional underbelly of social media and the rise of the social consumer isn't enough in itself to make your brand successful. So, in this book we're going to take a long journey together to uncover the secrets that will let you go beyond your preconceptions of broadcasting and marketing to build a successful and — yes, I'm saying it — *profitable* brand through Twitter. After all, you want to communicate with your consumers, understand what they want, and view your offerings from their perspective.

But first you have to learn to identify what tickles their emotions, what gets the conversation going, and what makes them respond with conviction and passion.

Unlike Heinz and those other brands of yesteryear, today's brands can't hide behind their logos. Nowadays, consumers want to know who they are. They don't want to talk to a faceless, nameless entity; they want to sense the person behind it — the personal. They want to like and get to know *you*, not just interact with your business. Having a friendly, smiling face in your Twitter profile is definitely more personal than just a logo. In essence, social media has dissolved the walls that existed between the consumer and the brand and has provided the opportunity for one-on-one connection in a way never before possible.

It's time to stop thinking of business as something cold, functional, and without a heartbeat. After all the very essence of business is the fulfilling of needs — a very personal and heartfelt thing, indeed. Once you fully grasp this concept, trust me, that proverbial lightbulb *will* turn on — and it will all make sense. It doesn't matter what your core business is — I'm not telling you what you should and shouldn't be selling,; you're smart enough to have figured that part out already. It's the *doing* that's drawn you to open these pages — the how and why and what's next of it all.

In a way, it's like show business! That first tweet is tantamount to that first opening performance. You've listened to the other acts perform, you've heard the audience's response, and now it's your turn. That all-important first tweet can be as nerve-wracking as a soliloquy.

Every morning my Twitter audience tune into my personal show. I comment on tweets I received and always retweet posts of interest that my audience has provided, along with my own comments. I suggest links that my audience may find interesting and, above all, I entertain them and keep them coming back for more. The @grattongirl brand has

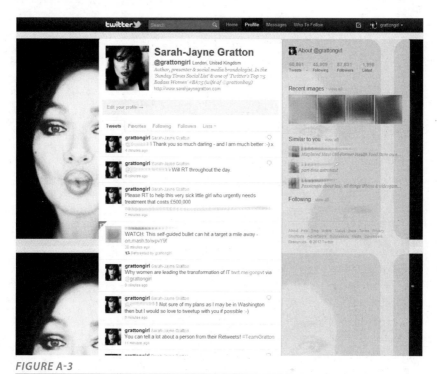

FIGURE A-3

Thousands feel connected to the @grattongirl brand.

become something that thousands have bonded with and feel connected to (see Figure A-3). As a result, my revenue streams have flourished, and both my pockets and my heart are full. I couldn't possibly have achieved this level of success using traditional forms of marketing — and neither can you.

I'm here to reveal how to create a brand that hits the ground running and how to evolve an existing brand into one that touches the hearts and lives of others.

And I'm not exaggerating! Remember that emotions are everything — they always have been and they always will be. Without them, we cease to be human and we cease to invest in the human race.

Read on, and remember that your journey starts here.

Part One

Twitter, You've Come a Long Way

We have an innate need to be a part of
something greater than ourselves and to
play a part in the events that shape
our worlds.

The Power of Twitter

This first part of the book is what I like to think of as a wake-up call as to what Twitter's all about and, more important, how essential it has become as a platform for today's personal brand.

I don't give the usual history lesson so I can instead focus on how Twitter has developed to become a force to be reckoned with.

It's a force that has transformed how we choose to communicate and source our information, one that has extended our possibilities for real-time connection and influence through communal discovery.

Twitter has evolved far beyond Jack Dorsey's vision of an SMS service on steroids. It has been shaped by the users themselves to incorporate and accomplish levels of social cohesion previously unimaginable.

So start your personal branding journey here, as I unveil both the visible and the hidden powers of Twitter.

"That I am touch'd with madness!
Make not impossible that which seems unlike:
'tis not impossible."

—*Measure for Measure*

1

A Twitter-Centric Landscape

And for some it was just that; a decent into madness.

I was one of those people who, like so many, found my introduction to Twitter a perplexing one. I couldn't quite get my head around why I would need a service that would allow me to send a message alerting others about my particular choice of breakfast cereal. An ideology based around what's basically an online SMS service? Madness indeed!

To Tweet — Perchance to Dream

The one thing you can say for certain about Twitter is that it makes a terrible first impression. But, as millions have discovered, it turns out that Twitter has an unexpected depth, coined by the writer Clive Thompson, as "ambient awareness." A strangely satisfying glimpse into those naked social segments of others, like a virtual peephole; but one where the observer knows he's being watched and enjoys the attention.

Twitter has dramatically transformed the way in which new ideas are shared and spread. News and information that would traditionally have taken hours, days, or even weeks to go from one location to another can now occur in seconds Twitter's power is both an ally to democracy and a mortal enemy to those governments and corporate entities who have created and held on to their power by controlling the information we mere mortals receive.

Because of the power of the tweet, the spreading of an idea, or of news occurring somewhere in the world can no longer be blocked. During the Iranian elections, for example, the Iranian government attempted to control communication and block any images of what was occurring in Iran from making their way to the general public. But they were never able to control all the information and images that were being seen by the world in real-time. Similarly, when an earthquake rocked the country of Haiti, not only were images from the torn country in the aftermath of the quake being tweeted around the world, but commentaries and opinions of what people were seeing were being read, heard, and readily retweeted.

Let's face it, the psychology of Twitter's appeal is enough, in itself, for a volume or two, but what's turned out to be the most interesting aspect of the platform is the way in which it's been embraced and expanded at such an extraordinary speed, to provide functionality that its creators never dreamed of. It's not only about what Twitter's doing to us anymore; it's about what we're doing to it!

The Shaping of the Personal Twitterverse

It's hard to comprehend that, when Twitter was first launched as a platform, there was no personal reply system in place. In fact, it was the early adopters' desire to reply to individual users that first created the @username tweets that are now a fundamental part of the service. Twitter had always been intended to be social but now it was becoming personal.

The other hugely important key to Twitter's continuing growth lies in the popularity of its application programming interface, or API, which allows programmers to develop software that interacts with Twitter.

Suddenly there was a need to tweet about anything and everything. New Twitter applications made it possible for unborn babies to tweet from inside the womb and for houseplants to tweet when they needed watering. All at once, the possibilities for connection seemed limitless and we found ourselves wondering how we every survived without it.

One of the biggest wake-up calls to the developers regarding what Twitter was capable of was brought about by the adoption of the API into an online Twitter search engine called Summize (see Figure 1-1). The program came up with a clever way of peering through Twitter's vast data stream using keywords — topic, person, or location-based — to find out what was being shared about them, and could be used to show contextual advertising along with the results it produced. Summize's ability to monetize conversations without being intrusive was something

FIGURE 1-1

Summize allowed users to search Twitter in real-time to provide greater value to the platform.

of a "Eureka!" moment for Twitter, which immediately saw a new revenue direction for the platform and took no time at all in purchasing Summize, along with its ideas.

Communal Discovery: For Better or for Worse

Another incredibly powerful way in which Twitter has been shaped by the public to become far more personal is by that great influencer: communal discovery. We have an innate need to be a part of something greater than ourselves and to play a part in the events that shape our worlds. The ability for the platform to be used to unite common causes for good is a monumental one, but to any positive there is a negative force (akin to good versus evil). For Twitter, that negativity came in the form of it being used to spread discontent and a call to violent action amongst a particular group of its users. In the case of the London riots of 2011, Twitter was accused of provoking the rioters into action by allowing them to converse and rile their intentions through their tweets. But what is even more interesting is how Twitter was also used to disprove many rumors.

"Tiger has been let out of London Zoo and is now loose in Camden. Not joking," tweeted one user, embellishing a story that rioters had released some of the animals at the London Zoo.

"They're burning down London Eye!!!! This is too much!!!!!!!!!!!" tweeted another, upon seeing a photograph appearing to show flames licking around the base of the South Bank landmark.

The *Guardian* newspaper, together with a team of researchers at the University of Manchester in England, analyzed seven rumors that emerged through Twitter during the five-day period of the London riots. These rumors ranged from the frivolous (that rioters had broken into and started cooking their own food at a McDonald's) to the more sober (the riots started as a result of police beating a 16-year-old girl).

Twitter provided a database of 2.6 million riot-related tweets to "Reading the Riots," an investigation into the summer disorder by the *Guardian* and London School of Economics. The study found that, contrary to widespread speculation at the time, Twitter was not used by rioters to incite or organize the disturbances. The finding called into question why so many people, from the prime minister to the acting head of the metropolitan police, blamed Twitter for spreading the disorder, even raising the prospect of closing it down at times of crisis. In fact,

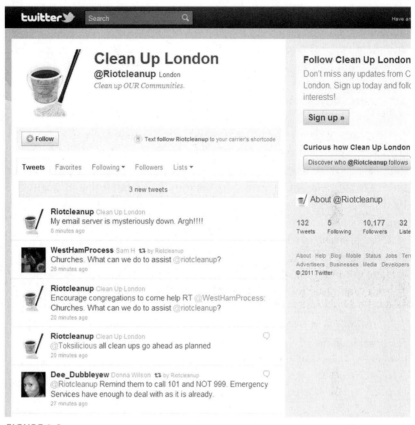

FIGURE 1-2

The Clean Up London Twitter Campaign

Twitter had a far more powerful effect for good during the time of the riots. It mobilized large numbers of people to the streets when it was used to organize a clean-up of riot-damaged streets.

Shortly after midnight on Tuesday, August 9, 2011, in the middle of the third night of rioting, Dan Thompson, a Worthing-based artist (who tweets as @artistsmakers) suggested Twitter users should take to the streets the following morning to help clear up the damage caused by the night's rioting under the Twitter name @Riotcleanup (see Figure 1-2).

The idea soon dwarfed coverage of the night's riots. More than 12,000 people posted messages asking for the people's help under the hashtag #riotcleanup, which were then retweeted more than 31,000 times, reaching more than 7 million users. And come the people did, in the thousands, with people from all walks of life pitching in. An offer of help from handyman service @The_Multiman: "#riotcleanup if you have a shop or home that has been affected my handymen will volunteer in our spare time to help with any repairs! Pls RT" was indeed retweeted 2,980 times, demonstrating just how effective proactive community discovery through Twitter can be.

The face of communication has and is continuing to evolve. Once scattered communities are now uniting through social media to make themselves heard. A great example of this can be found in the health care service, where patient's frustration has found a united voice through Twitter. Not content with the long hours spent in hospital and doctors' waiting rooms, tired of the endless government cutbacks that have resulted in a decrease in all important health care services and staff, patients have taken to Twitter to voice their frustration with great effect. And it's not just the patients! Doctors too, such as MDs Howard Luks (@hjluks) and Kevin Pho (@kevinmd) have found a great ally in Twitter. They use it as a means of reaching out to their patients and empowering them through a stream of information and knowledge that they could never achieve on a one-on-one basis. They've seen Twitter as a way to reach thousands, even millions in a way that adds true value to their lives.

Tweeting Outside the Box

One of the things I most love above Twitter, for personal branding, is the fact that its effectiveness has nothing to do with your bank balance but with those sparks of creativity that drive us to think outside the proverbial box and make a real impact online. I've found amazing stories about how Twitter has helped turn dying businesses and brands around with little to no financial investment. Here are some examples that I like to share with new users that haven't yet discovered Twitter's power.

Aaron Durand's mother was panicking! Her beloved Broadway Books, an independent bookstore in Portland, Oregon, she had run for almost two decades, had fallen on hard times due to the economic downturn and her shop was being threatened with closure. Aaron desperately wanted to do something to help turn things around, but wasn't sure what. First he blogged about his mother's plight but then he decided to tweet

if you're in Portland do me a favor??? Buy a book at Broadway Books. No wait, buy 3 of em. I'll buy you a burrito the next time I'm in town.

FIGURE 1-3

A simple tweet can change the destiny of a brand.

it, adding that he would buy a burrito for anyone who bought $50 or more worth of books at his mom's shop during the holiday season (see Figure 1-3).

Aaron certainly didn't expect the story to take off the way it did. Within hours, it had been retweeted thousands of times across Portland's art and design community and, overnight, new customers started to arrive at the bookstore. The story continued to grow on Twitter thanks to Aaron's creativity and his ability to connect in a way that drew the support of the entire community. Consequently his mother's bookstore went on to have the best holiday season ever, and it is still going strong.

When Peter Shankland sent out his tweet to Morton's Steakhouse, he expected nothing to come of it. Weary from his endless meetings and craving his favorite food, he tweeted a request to the company from the airport just before he boarded his flight, jokingly requesting that they meet him with a steak when he landed. He heard nothing back from the restaurant but, upon landing, was amazed see a tuxedo-clad Morton's waiter at the arrival gate with steak, shrimp, a side of potatoes, bread, two napkins, and silverware.

Morton's truly understands the power of Twitter and has used it to great advantage for its brand.

The event was tweeted and retweeted thousands of times, resulting in Morton's Steakhouse experiencing a massive increase in profits over the following 12 months.

Now there's an example of a company that really listens and responds to its customer's needs!

I'm not saying that you need to dash out the door with freebies for everyone who tweets about you. What I want you to draw from these brand stories is the importance of taking your Twitter followers seriously and understanding the social power they carry for your brand across what has become a Twitter-centric landscape.

Twitter allows us to become both commander and editor of our personal world; to dissect the information that we choose to receive each day and to reshape it into patterns that best define our own value propositions.

Twitter newbies, however, won't immediately comprehend how it's possible to effectively curate through the tidal wave of tweets that crash down on their screens every second. There's a lot of social media noise out there and it can seem an endlessly daunting task to filter and tune it into sections of information that are meaningful for you and, in turn, will prove to be meaningful to others. I'm going to show you the secrets of becoming a great curator and the best ways to segment and categorize those tweets into value-nuggets that you can use as a promotional funnel for brand "you."

"Would you have been so brief with him,
he would have been so brief with you; to shorten you."

—*King Richard II*

2

'Less' Is the New 'More'

When I was first asked to comment on how much Twitter has contributed to the rise of the personal brand, a particular quote immediately sprang to mind; a quote usually attributed to Mark Twain, although actually written by Blaise Pascal:

"I would have written a shorter letter, but I did not have the time."

It's a profound and an oh so true statement about how Twitter has been able to boil down content to its true core message — and the same is true for your brand and its core message.

Sorting the Wheat from the Chaff

These days, information is fast-flowing and constant, and it has become increasingly hard to sort the wheat from the chaff in terms of what adds value to both my businesses and myself. I find lengthy articles best saved for those bedtime reading moments that increasingly never seem to come, as all too often I fall into bed in the wee small hours, when reading is the furthest thing from my exhausted mind.

It is a scientifically proven fact that how we read content has changed due to the evolution of how information reaches us and the speed with which it does so. And the change isn't a recent one. As far back as 1997, Jakob Nielsen of Alertbox was researching the way that people read web pages. What he discovered is that, in fact, we don't! Instead we scan, picking out individual words and sentences. In Nielsen's research, he discovered that 79 percent of his test readers always scanned new pages and only 16 percent read word by word. Nielsen continued his studies and, in 2010, found that this figure had increased to 83 percent, and even further to 85 percent when information was received via mobile devices.

As a result, web pages had to use "scannable" text, using:

- ▶ highlighted keywords (hypertext links serve as a form of highlighting; typeface variations and color are other methods)
- ▶ meaningful subheadings (not "clever" ones)
- ▶ bulleted lists
- ▶ one idea per paragraph (users skip over any additional ideas if they are not caught by the first few words in the paragraph)
- ▶ inverted pyramid style, starting with the conclusion
- ▶ half (or less) the word count than conventional writing

When you incorporate reader style into the content you build, you begin to see how Twitter is a great ally to your brand in ensuring you master the art of succinct and disciplined content.

In my postgrad student years, when I first started promoting my one-act plays to drama societies, I remember attending a lecture given by the eminent playwright Alyn Aykborn at the University of Wales in Cardiff, South Wales. I sat in awe as he talked about his approach to scene dialog and, again, the virtues of the "less is more" philosophy to writing. He said that he never added to his work but, instead, subtracted, to apply more meaning and resonance to his plays. He reminded the class that it's not what you put in but what you can take out that provides the most power for the audience. Looking back at the lecture, he could very well have been talking about writing for Twitter.

The World in Our Pockets

And then there's the mobile element. The way society increasingly chooses to receive its content on the move is driven by our incessant need for speed and the concept that there are just never enough hours in the day. These are major contributing factors to Twitter's phenomenal success and the reason that its power continues to grow. We need our world to be portable; one that we can carry in our pockets. It's up to the brands themselves to communicate in a way that resonates most with their audience by clever curation and tweet construction.

My husband, Dr. Dean Anthony Gratton, coined the term "the Lawnmower Man Effect" (see Figure 2-1) to explain this very shift in his book *The Handbook of Personal Area Networking Technologies and Protocols* (Cambridge University Press, 2012).

He wrote, "The Lawnmower Man Effect (LME) represents the consumers' ability to traverse digital systems across the globe all

FIGURE 2-1

A graphic representation of the Lawnmower Man Effect (courtesy of Cambridge University Press)

captained from their personal area networking space utilizing pervasive WAN technologies."

The term is used to describe the need we have to be "intrinsically-connected" to our world through technology. It came about as a result of our weekly Friday movie-night ritual, where one of us each week chooses a different (and sometimes obscure) movie from their childhood to watch over a chili and taco supper. We had tuned into my choice of the 1980s movie *The Lawnmower Man* this particular Friday; where the brilliant scientist, played by Pierce Brosnan, subjects the imbecile gardener, played by Jeff Farley, to a series of experiments that transform him from blithering idiot to mind-blowing genius in a matter of weeks. The movie takes a malevolent turn however, as all good Friday-night movies do,

Mallary Tenore
@mallarytenore

Following

Join us now for a live chat about how reporters can take a watchdog approach when reporting on veterans affairs: journ.us/zkjXk8

4:51 PM - 15 Feb 12 via TweetDeck · Embed this Tweet
← Reply ↑↓ Retweet ★ Favorite ≋ Buffer

FIGURE 2-2

Writer Mallary Jean Tenore has found Twitter to be an asset to her writing style.

when our newly created Einstein turns into a fiendishly knowledge hungry monster and eventually evolves to become a malignant part of the technology itself.

I was happily crunching my taco to the sound of Brosnan's screams when the whoop of joy beside me indicated that hubby had experienced another of his "Eureka!" moments in finding the perfect example on which to coin his latest theory.

Journalism has been forced to wake up and respond to these changes. Some writers have embraced them, while others have rejected their appeal, hoping against hope that the platform will die and society will return to, what they consider to be its former glory days.

An associate editor at Poynter.org, Mallary Jean Tenore, has found Twitter to be a great asset to her writing (see Figure 2-2). She explains, "Twitter taught me that, in writing, every word counts (literally). By limiting myself to 140 characters, I have to be strategic about how many words I use and how I use them. Training myself to write succinctly on Twitter has made me more aware of extra words in my stories.

"I've cut down the clutter, but still tend to be wordy when I'm unsure of what I want to say, or when I'm tired and preoccupied. I recently started a new experiment to help with this. As time allows, I read through my stories before submitting them and read every sentence as if it were a tweet. How would I write this sentence if I were tweeting it? Are there words I could cut that would save space but not change the meaning of what I'm saying? If so, I start trimming."

Spring-Cleaning Your Brand Approach

One of Twitter's greatest gifts to brands lies in its simplicity. It enables us to cut through the clutter and fine-tune our content, along with the way that we share it with our audience, by focusing on what really matters to us and to them. Gone are the sugarcoating and marshmallow padding of those corporate promotions of old. It's time to revamp brand "us" and clean up our online act so that every Twitter message not only reflects us, but the value that our brand can offer to others.

Once you've learned how to maximize your brand dialog by minimizing its content, you can use the architecture of the perfect Twitter formula that I explain in Chapter 5. It's a unique method that brings together all the essential elements you need to create a sustainable brand impact each and every day regardless of location, and it's one that works for your brand around the clock to ensure that your tweets keep your audience retweeting and coming back for more.

In Part Two, you learn how to adopt literally thousands of brand ambassadors; those loyal followers who work to promote brand "you" every day.

I lead you through everything you need to know to translate your personal statement onto Twitter and to nurture it through cross-platform promotion, landing page primers, and other never-before-revealed secrets to success.

I also show you how to translate your brand message globally across a variety of different cultures and philosophies; something that's vital for worldwide success.

So read on and let's get building brand "you."

Part Two

Creating and Showcasing Your Brand

IN THIS PART

The most successful personal brands are those that simplify the complexity of today's Twitter-fueled information overload and provide a safe haven amid the chaos.

It's All about You

So, we move on to the subject of "you." It's time to get serious defining and shaping your personal brand. This part starts with a few simple exercises that will leave you with a clear understanding of your personal brand message, something that's an essential element to building an effective personal brand on Twitter.

I explain how to charge your personal brand with emotional equity and show you how to produce true value in a crowded marketplace where emotions rule our purchasing decisions on a subconscious level every day.

I reveal the key influence strengtheners you need to know to keep ahead of the competition in your arena, and I take you step by step through the secrets of building a great Twitter profile.

I also teach you the four types of tweet you need to use each day to quickly build your popularity and influence across the Twitterverse, show you how to attract large numbers of quality followers, and explain how to translate your personal brand message into your very own 24-hour Twitter brand show.

"This above all; to thine ownself be true."

—*Hamlet*

3

Building Brand 'You'

For those of you doubting the existence of the personal brand or asking yourself, "Why should I care about this branding stuff? It doesn't apply to me or what I do?" let me provide you with a stark reality check.

We live in an age where a potential employer will Google you before even inviting you to an interview where, in all your interactions, both offline and on, your virtual reputation precedes your physical one 99 percent of the time.

Whether you're still a student, looking for work, an entrepreneur, or an employee in a global corporation, you need to start thinking, acting, and planning like a leader and take control of brand "you."

In the ever-evolving spectrum of social media, you have to learn how to master the ability to manage your online reputation. You need to be in control of all those impressions of you and to build on them in a way that will ensure your future success.

Your personal brand is all about who you are and what you want to be known for on an emotional, introspective level. You need to begin your journey with your eyes wide open and with a clear vision of your unique and very personal promise of value.

Your Personal Brand Statement

This is an exercise I like to do with every client I work with and I'm going to share it with you now:

Write your personal brand statement in 140 characters or less!

It's more difficult than it looks and will be distinctive to you and you alone. But what exactly is a personal brand statement?

The answer is that it is a statement that succinctly communications what you're best at (*your brand value*), who you provide it to (*your brand audience*), and how you provide it (*your delivery method*).

After all, your personal brand statement is far more than a label, a job title, or a mission statement. And it's not a bottom-line prophecy about your long-term career and life objectives. Don't think of it in corporate terms but instead approach it from the inside out, because before you can start promoting brand "you," you need to fine-tune your own understanding of exactly who brand "you" is.

When putting together your personal brand statement, remember to be absolutely clear on the value you provide to others and don't confuse them by using woolly terms that really don't mean anything. Stay focused on your area of expertise and remember that nobody wants to invest in a jack of trades, master of none.

Stay authentic, but don't be afraid to dream a little. By this I mean that you shouldn't be afraid to express your inner strengths in the statement, even if you have not yet flexed their virtual muscle, provided you know that they are genuine.

That old Einstein saying has never been truer than in the personal branding arena: "You do not really understand something unless you can explain it to your grandmother." So, when constructing your personal brand statement, avoid using technical words or industry jargon that could alienate your audience. If your grandmother can understand it then so will your followers.

Understanding Your Emotional Value Keys

Step outside yourself for a moment and think about how your personality affects the experience someone will have with you from his or her perspective. For example, are you amazingly organized? Do people love working with you for your ability to empathize with others, or for your wonderful sense of humor? Now write down those words that best describe these assets of your personality. These are your *emotional value keys*.

Here are the key questions to ask yourself:

▶ How am I described by others?

FIGURE 3-1

@grattongirl's personal brand statement

- How would I like others to describe me?
- What benefit do I give to others?
- How do I provide these benefits?
- What benefits would I like to provide?
- What do I have that makes me stand out from everyone else?

Now pick five key words from your list, those that most clearly communicate who you are. The result should read like an inspiring mantra — either a *being* one, as in a "dependable, creative professional connector" or a *doing* one, such as "always motivating others to do their best."

Now you have the five emotional value keys necessary to construct your personal brand statement in 140 characters or less. When it's set down and embraced, not only will you start to see your personal brand in a whole new (and very personal) light, but so will your current and future followers.

My personal brand statement (see Figure 3-1) is a *doing* one, full of ambient social warmth that, over time, others have come to echo as my brand ambassadors.

Let's break my statement down to see the bare-bones of its construction: First, there is the word "delight," an emotional word that describes how feelings of satisfaction, warmth, and accomplishment motivate me to work on behalf of others. Second, the word "helping" is an important and powerful word that conjures up subconscious feelings of needs being fulfilled and support being given. Next, I talk about the creation and unleashing of personal brand identity, letting my target audience know exactly what I can offer and whetting their appetite for more information. Finally, I provide another audience indicator and a method of delivery, which is "on Twitter."

Your personal brand statement is the starting point from which your brand will be developed on Twitter. It must resonate warmth and convey to your audience the essence of who and what you are.

Your Brand Chemistry: The Vision, Value, Passion Connection

Another gift of the personal brand is the way it allows your potential clients, employers, and associates to look at your brand's "chemistry" to assess whether it's the right fit for their needs. Personal branding helps generate this chemistry for you by spotlighting your social warmth alongside your knowledge base and experience. People hire and work with people they like. They want people who will fit their corporate culture, so they want to know what kind of person you are. Your target audience expects nothing less than the whole package, and personal branding lets them see it more clearly.

So let's do more homework and undertake an exercise I like to call the Vision, Value, Passion (VVP) Connection (see Figure 3-2). Set aside at least an hour for the exercise as it needs your absolute focus and attention to provide maximum benefits in building your brand.

Vision

What is your vision and your purpose in life? I want you to look at this question from both an external perspective (the bigger picture) and an internal perspective (how you are emotionally driven to it) to clarify exactly what is it and how you feel you might best realize it.

Now, think about one problem that you want to see transformed and improved in your life. What role might your vision play in solving this? On many occasions, the problem's solution often turns out to be the vision itself. Your role in making it happen is your purpose.

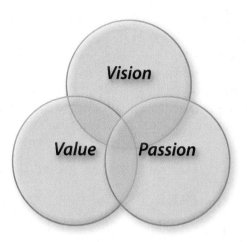

FIGURE 3-2

The Vision, Value, Passion (VVP) Connection

Value

What are your personal values, your moral boundaries, and your guiding principles? For example, honesty, integrity, sensitivity, enthusiasm, inner strength, and pride are all examples of the values we hold, both for ourselves and for others. Take time to write down your values.

Now, take time in defining where you feel your value system came from. One of the best methods of achieving this is through simple word association. It can take practice but word association can be a great tool in uncovering your inner belief system. Say each of your personal values aloud and write down the first word that comes into your head when you hear it, followed by the second, and then the third. Repeat this process for each of your values, and the results will surprise you.

The unconscious mind holds on to those core beliefs that drive our values every day, the ones that our conscious mind has filed away. This exercise helps you to unlock your values and is incredibly powerful and cathartic.

Passion

What fascinates you most? What activities, interests, and topics put a spring in your step and have you leaping out of bed at 6 a.m. on a Sunday morning, or talking about excitedly with others? Whether it's wine tasting, bungee jumping, music, theater, or ice hockey, write down all the things you are passionate about.

Now consider how your passions connect to the things you do best. Look at your personal statement and see how it ties in with your passions and interests. Every connection you come to see and understand is another brush stroke in the portrait of brand "you."

Charging Your Personal Brand with Emotional Equity

Remember that the emotional brain is far more powerful than the logical brain — we remember how people make us feel far more than we remember their actions. It is the feeling behind the doing that rules in life. Dawn Leijon, a professor of marketing at Georgetown University and former brand manager for Kraft, put it this way: "Branding isn't about logos, slogans, or advertising — those are just tools. Branding is about making people remember your organization, service, or product and what's unique about it."

Your brand resides in the minds, and hearts, of your customers, clients, connections, and prospects. It is the sum total of their experiences and perceptions, and can be influenced by many factors, all of which I will explain to you. Branding provides true social and revenue-based value in a crowded marketplace where emotions rule our purchasing decisions on a subconscious level every day.

Your brand is a promise to your customers. Its fabric is woven with your personal brand statement and should be threaded through all other aspects of your social and professional contact.

FIGURE 3-3

Magda Arnold's Appraisal Theory of Emotion

As a student of psychology, I was intrigued by Professor Magda Arnold's pioneering work in personality measurement, which began in 1946 and continued until her death in 2002. Arnold was convinced that personality measures were needed in addition to traditional intelligence tests to provide a complete picture of a person's abilities; a debate that is continuing to this day.

Her research and her Appraisal Theory of Emotion led me to better understand the circuitry of the brain that mediates sensation, perception, motivation, and emotion, an understanding which later triggered my fascination in consumer psychology and brand influence (see Figure 3-3)

FIGURE 3-4

Our knowledge becomes marked as either a positive or a negative internal image that controls our decision making.

Simply put, situations and events happen. We appraise them internally and it is ultimately the emotional effect they leave in us that determines the action we take. As far as your brand is concerned, this can be looked at as your emotional equity.

In 1994, the neuropsychologist Antonio Demasio theorized that thought is made up largely of internally constructed images based on symbolic and perceptual representation of the words, sounds, sights, and other stimuli we come into contact with every day. A lifetime of learning leads these images to become internally "marked" in either a positive or negative manner that affects, not only the conclusions we draw, but the future outcomes we decide on (see Figure 3-4).

For example, when a "negative" image is linked with a potential decision, it sounds a form of unconscious internal alarm, which deters us from taking that route, whereas, stimuli resulting in a "positive" image being linked to an outcome becomes an internal beacon of incentive.

How do we charge our brands with emotional equity? It certainly won't happen overnight; it's a long-term and ongoing process. But certain key findings have been made in providing an emotional trigger through our brand content and its correlation to long-term brand success and sustainability.

Maybe There Is Something in All Those Kitten Pictures

In 1999, Jennifer L. Harris, John A. Bargh, and Kelly D. Brownell from Yale University carried out experiments to test the hypothesis that exposure to food imagery during television viewing may contribute to obesity by triggering automatic snacking of available food.

In Experiments 1a and 1b, elementary-school-age children watched a cartoon that contained either food images or images of other products and received a snack while watching. In Experiment 2, three groups of adults watched either a television program that included food images that associated snacking with fun, food images that showed nutrition benefits of healthy eating, or no food images whatsoever. The adults then tasted and evaluated a range of healthy to unhealthy snack foods in an apparently separate experiment.

The outcome compared the amount of snack foods consumed during and after the image exposure and found the following:

▶ Children consumed 45 percent more food when exposed to food images.

▶ Adults consumed more of both healthy and unhealthy snack foods following exposure to snack-food images compared to the group shown no food images.

▶ In both experiments, food imagery increased consumption of food intake, and these effects were not related to reported hunger or other conscious influences.

These experiments demonstrate the incredible power of imagery in influencing behavior when associated with a particular brand. They are a powerful knowledge primer when setting your brand content and building your followers.

Indeed, knowledge is power, but it's also a responsibility and a lesson in longevity, as the brands that survive the longest are the ones that actually deliver on their promises.

What's more, it's important to remember that the most successful personal brands are those that simplify the complexity of today's Twitter-fueled information overload and provide a safe haven amid the chaos. I will show you how to filter out the noise and offer specific and simple solutions.

Traditional advertising has always used emotional pulls to sell and promote, but through social media, these pulls have evolved into real-time emotional involvement, where we have the opportunity to proactively participate in our brands' worlds. We have a voice and we aren't afraid to use it as both consumers and advocates.

As mentioned in this book's introduction, this fact is a double-edged sword, as a bad customer service experience can be echoed to literally thousands in a matter of seconds. It is also an alert for personal brand creators to keep it real and to demonstrate integrity in the content they provide. It's about curation rather than manipulation.

Celebrities have found a way of echoing their personal brands. Thanks to Twitter, they can bypass the paparazzi by using the platform to post personal images and messages that reveal their true personality, offering their followers a glimpse of their lives off-screen, while imparting a sense of sharing private moments (see Figure 3-5).

rihanna Rihanna
Welcome to the world princess Carter! Love Aunty Rih
1 hour ago

UncleRUSH Russell Simmons
congrats to my good friends Beyonce and Jay-Z >> bit.ly/x13khb
1 hour ago

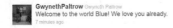

GwynethPaltrow Gwyneth Paltrow
Welcome to the world Blue! We love you already.
7 minutes ago

FIGURE 3-5

Beyoncé bypassed the paparazzi to tweet the first picture of her baby girl to her followers, and many celebrities tweeted back their congratulations

Many celebrities have learned through trial and error the good, the bad, and the ugly of what they choose to share. The clever ones have found a balance between the intimate and the public persona that manages to bring us closer to them without completely removing the mystery that made them stars.

Repeat after Me: Power Isn't a Dirty Word!

Creating brand "you" means coming to terms with power — your power! It's a word that's so misunderstood and, as a result, too often misused. Power has nothing to do with physical strength, tyranny, or who has the biggest office. I'm talking about the power of influence.

Which brings us back to the Vision, Value, Passion (VVP) Connection; those things you have already established as the building blocks of your brand and the essence of your personal brand statement. They contribute greatly to the power of your reputation and make you a highly influential and must-add follow.

On Twitter, this power is measured not only by the number of followers you have, but also by the amplification level of your tweets through retweets and acknowledgements. I answer the quality versus quantity question surrounding Twitter followers in Chapter 6, but for now I focus on the importance of unleashing and using your personal power intelligently, responsibly, and — yes you've guessed it — powerfully!

The Halo Effect

One of the things that attract us to certain brands is the power they project. As a consumer, you want to associate with brands whose powerful presence creates a halo effect that rubs off on you — and it's the same on Twitter. Remember that power is perception and that perception starts on an internal level. In other words, if you want others to see you as highly influential then you need to see yourself that way first.

After all, you are already a leader — you're leading brand "you," so you need to ensure that your Twitter presence recognizes this and influence others to follow.

I have identified seven key influence strengtheners for your personal brand on Twitter, which I introduce here and expand on extensively throughout the book.

1. Keep the home fires burning

Don't neglect your personal brand's website, and do ensure that it resonates with the passion of your personal brand statement. Whether you create it yourself or pay a professional website company to design it, having an approachable and clean online home base for both your professional and social streams is a necessity.

As you are the brand itself, the best domain you can acquire is your first and last name, or something close to it.

However, this can be difficult, as website domains are being picked up like candy and finding your own name is often impossible, especially if it is a common one like Smith or Jones. Luckily, I was able to secure www.sarahjaynegratton.com a few years ago, but it's always a good idea to have some well-thought-out backup names just in case. Play around with terms that define you as a brand and that echo your personal brand statement. These terms will also make excellent domain names for your website.

2. Keep blogging sharable content

Although so-called online experts regularly declare that blogging is dead, I believe blogging has simply evolved and become far more diverse. It is no longer necessary to write multiparagraph posts; instead, services such as Tumblr and Posterous Spaces make it easy for individuals to share shorter entries or snippets of text that often include photos and other media, or to use their Twitter accounts to generate self-sustaining blogs that show what's trending for their personal brand (see Figure 3-6).

Remember that sharable content is a great influence strengthener for your personal brand, steering your Twitter audience to it, and establishing yourself as an expert in your field.

3. Avoid mobile mistakes

In November 2011, top tweeter Ashton Kutcher posted a tweet defending Penn State's Joe Paterno without doing his homework about the sex-abuse controversy surrounding the coach (see Figure 3-7). His tweet resulted in a catastrophic frenzy of furious replies from Kutcher's millions of followers. Once again, this is a prime example of how 140 characters or less can immediately damage someone's reputation and subsequently their personal brand.

FIGURE 3-6

Twylah translates your tweets into a uniquely personalized blog page

How do you fire Jo Pa? #insult #noclass as
a hawkeye fan I find it in poor taste

FIGURE 3-7

Ashton Kutcher's badly thought-out Twitter post resulted in a frenzy of furious
replies.

With more and more of us tweeting from our cell phones, it's far too
easy to make a real-time mistake like this; whether it's updating your
status with an inappropriate comment or letting auto-correct do digital
damage. In other words, when networking on the go make sure you
carefully review what you are about to tweet before pushing that Send
button.

4. Interaction, interaction, interaction!

Take a look at the most popular noncelebrity personal brands on
Twitter and see how frequently they interact with their followers. You'll
find that if they're not sharing great content, they are either responding
to messages or retweeting their followers to keep the conversation going.

And it doesn't have to be a full-time job. A carefully thought-out
Twitter strategy can provide the interaction your brand needs without
taking up too much of your valuable time.

Chapter 5 reveals the secrets to building a strong and trusted Twitter
dialog for your brand. By learning both the architecture and the formula
needed to create great tweets on a daily basis, you will quickly build your
popularity and influence across the Twitterverse.

Remember, there has been a shift from a monolog-based to a dialog-
based approach to brand promotion (see Figure 3-8). Your followers are
an integral part of your brand content. Keep them involved and they will
increase in number.

5. Use hashtags

Hashtags might be one of the hardest things for new Twitter users to
learn, but they are invaluable. The hashtag, or the # symbol, is used on

FIGURE 3-8

An example of Twitter dialog communication that has replaced the older mono-logue forms of brand promotion.

Twitter to tag a topic or keyword in a tweet. The most popular are known as trending topics.

A great example of how powerful hashtags can be is that just seconds after Beyoncé and Jay-Z's name for their new baby girl was incorrectly announced as Ivy Blue, the Twitter hashtags #IvyBlue and #NamesBetterThanIvyBlue were created, with hundreds of tweets flowing about the strange choice of baby's name, and making them instantly trending topics. Of course, these hashtags were created when it was thought that the baby's name was Ivy Blue. Later, the hashtag was changed to #BlueIvy.

Close friends of Beyoncé and Jay-Z tweeted their congratulations to share their well-wishes, not only with the new parents, but with their followers, too. Gwyneth Paltrow (@GwynethPaltrow) tweeted, "Welcome to the world, Blue! We love you already."

By learning how to use the right hashtags, your tweets can reach a far larger audience and, as a result, substantially increase your influence. But knowing how to create trending topics that will really make an impact is something of a mystery. I lift the lid and reveal everything you need to know about creating them in Chapter 10.

Figure 3-9 shows how Twitter has evolved its hashtag search through its Discover pane, along with a list of Worldwide Trends on the home page.

6. Create lists and get listed

Twitter offers you the ability to create extensive lists composed of other Twitter users. These lists categorize users by the topics they cover, becoming invaluable depositories of information on various subjects.

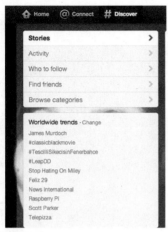

FIGURE 3-9

Twitter has evolved its hashtag search facility through the introduction of the Discover pane.

Creating lists that relate to what you enjoy or tweet about can help spread your influence on Twitter, both with the people included on your lists and anyone looking for tweets on those subjects.

As you become known as an expert in your field, you will be listed time and time again in subject relevant lists and, on a wider level, through the kind of tweeter you are, in lists such as Follow, Top Tweeters, Influential Women, Visionaries, Inspirational, and other lists that single you out as someone with a great deal of influence and who's an essential follow. Figure 3-10 shows a snapshot of some of the lists that feature the @grattongirl brand. In Chapter 6, I explain how to create lists that get plenty of attention and, likewise, how to ensure your personal brand is listed again and again.

7. Timing is everything

Knowing the best time of the day to tweet can be something of an art form, but fortunately there are tools available that enable you to reach your global following at the best possible times of day. The question is no longer "Should we spend our time on Twitter?" but "How can we optimize our time on Twitter?"

And the key to maximizing your return from Twitter really comes down to timing your tweets for success. This means getting to know your

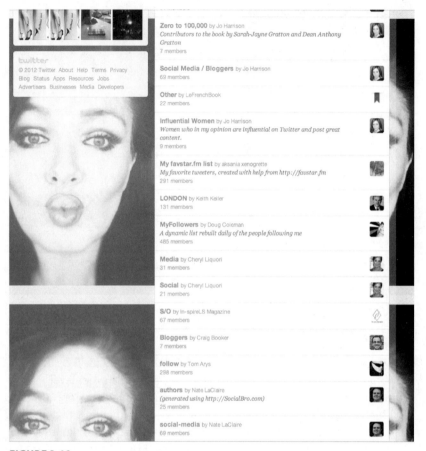

FIGURE 3-10

Just a few of the many lists that feature the @grattongirl brand on Twitter.

audience and understanding the differences between time zones when planning your tweet schedules. It's also a great way to incorporate Twitter lists, allowing you to group followers according to time zone and peak Twitter periods.

As the book progresses, you'll learn all you need to know about maximizing your tweet timing for greater exposure and increased influence.

So, now you've learned the importance of giving your personal brand a strong voice from the start. The next step is to transform your voice into a great Twitter profile; one that truly lets it shine and quickly attracts a strong and loyal following. The next chapters show you how to achieve this profile in just minutes.

So what are you waiting for? Let's start building your personal brand profile!

"You are a gentleman of excellent breeding, admirable discourse, of great admittance, authentic in your place and person."

—*Merry Wives of Windsor*

4

Secrets of a Great Twitter Profile

It all starts with your profile picture, the one that says, "This is what I'm all about."

It's the first thing your potential followers will see, so it needs to have a serious wow factor but not necessarily big-bucks investment. Some of the best profile shots happen by accident; in fact you may already have the perfect profile picture on your hard disk. It's the one that instantly says all it needs to about your personal brand.

Thinking Outside the Box

This chapter isn't about giving you a photography lesson; it's all about making you think outside the box about how you present your brand to others. I was chatting with a photographer recently who told me about a personal brand portrait shoot he had done with a businessman at his home. He had taken many head and shoulder shots — shots at the client's desk, shots in front of framed degrees, and other corporate-type images. They had all turned out fairly standard — none really stood out from the crowd.

The photographer and the subject agreed that there were plenty of usable shots but they wanted to create something special and out of the box. The photographer suggested they try some jumping shots. The subject was hesitant at first but stepped out of his comfort zone and, dressed in his suit and tie, started jumping! The shots were amazing, surprising, and quite funny. The shoot culminated with the subject jumping in his pool for one last image!

Although this might all sound a little silly, the shots ended up being featured in a magazine spread about the businessman. It was the series of out-of-the-box images that convinced the magazine he was someone that it would want to feature.

FIGURE 4-1

Forget expensive photo shoots — adding an effect such as texture, lo-mo, or sketch (available on most photo-editing software) to a home-taken headshot can give it a completely different feel.

Try playing around with some of the great free photo-editing resources available today on a good-quality shot of yourself and see how altering focus, color, or other effects can change the statement of a bland head-and-shoulders shot, as Figure 4-1 shows.

The Search Engine Optimization (SEO) Trick

Once you've chosen your picture, there's a clever trick you can use to ensure that your photo is optimized for maximum recognition. I'm talking about a unique search engine optimization (SEO) trick that not many people are aware of. It's simple: Although you can't add tags to your photo, you can rename it before you upload, using keywords that will help identify your brand to others and draw people toward you. Doing that means that when your photo appears in the URL, it will contain the keywords you selected. A word of warning: Don't use spaces when adding your keywords as they will make the link more difficult to translate, and it may not show up easily during a search.

The Power of First Impressions

People don't merely form first impressions; they become attached to them. Social scientists have given this phenomenon a name: the Fundamental Attribution Error (FAE). It is a term that gives credence to the cliché "You never get a second chance to make a first impression" and it stems from the fact that people are complex. To simplify this complexity, we have a tendency to pigeonhole one another into specific categories after only the briefest of interactions. For example, someone who observes an athlete signing autographs on one occasion will probably assume the athlete is a nice person. In reality, there are many other aspects to that athlete's personality. But to make life simpler, we tend to conclude that she is a nice person.

This internal categorization has its positives and negatives. On the positive side, if you really wow enough people with your first impression, you can coast on the momentum of that powerful first impression for a long, long time.

But the principle of FAE can also prove to be fatal. Suppose someone catches you on a bad day. If you are not careful, your personal brand could be severely marred. How many actors and athletes have been branded as arrogant because they preferred not to sign an autograph in a restaurant while eating with their family?

It is an unavoidable reality that we make snap judgments about others based on a fraction of the relevant information. Building a great personal brand ensures you make the principle of FAE work for you, rather than against you.

Getting a Handle on Your Handle

In terms of your personal brand, clearly your best possible Twitter account handle is your own name. However, if you have a common name, such as Smith or Jones, you may find it has already been taken. Try different variations, or adding a middle initial if you have one.

You can also separate parts of your name with an underscore, for example, Anna Louise Smith could become the Twitter handle @AnnaSmith, @AnnaLouiseSmith, or @AnnaLSmith, or it could be broken up using the underscore to make the handles @Anna_Smith, @Anna_L_Smith, or even @AnnaSmith_.

Alternatively, and here's where you need to get creative, you can choose to experiment with alternatives that incorporate your name and personal brand statement. For example, if Anna Smith is an artist, she could use the handle @AnnaSmithArtist or even @AnnaLovesArt.

When Marcella Selbach started her Independent Movies Promotional Services, she wanted her Twitter handle to immediately portray what she was all about to her followers. The name @movieangel was the perfect choice and is synonymous with support and help for independent movies makers around the globe. She also used the name in her website (www.

FIGURE 4-2

Marcella Selbach's personal branding as @movieangel on Twitter

movieangel.net) and chose a golden roll of film as her profile picture, again strengthening her brand message. She then chose to feature herself in the background image to illustrate her personal passion for movies and to humanize her profile page further, as Figure 4-2 shows.

Deciding to use the name @movieangel was a clever move as it also incorporates the keyword that Marcella wanted to rank highly in. In other words, when people search the word "movie" in Twitter, @movieangel will be in the results. There are many possible Twitter handle combinations, so it's important to take some time in choosing the right one for you.

One thing to bear in mind in this process is the 140-character limit that Twitter imposes. If you choose a long Twitter handle, you leave less room for message content and replies. Twitter currently limits usernames to 15 characters or less for this very reason.

Trust Your Instincts

My Twitter handle, @grattongirl (see Figure 4-3), came about as a result of wanting to showcase my personal brand through Twitter without using my full name, which would have been way too long. As a writer, having my surname as part of my handle was important to me, so

FIGURE 4-3

My @grattongirl Twitter profile page

I played around with various alternatives and @grattongirl just felt right. Don't be afraid to use your instincts and choose a name that speaks to you internally.

Soon afterwards, my husband, Dean Anthony Gratton, joined Twitter as @grattonboy. Our husband-and-wife profiles worked in harmony to promote our individual brands as well as inadvertently creating a further brand, #teamgratton, which I explain more about in Chapter 10.

Bring on the Bio

The good news is that your bio is already 90 percent written in the form of your personal brand statement, which I showed you how to put together in Chapter 3. All you need to add now is your website's URL to draw people even closer into brand "you." Thus, it's worth taking the time to make sure your website lives up to your brand's message and audience expectations.

You can also add your location if what you are offering is area-specific (see Figure 4-4).

FIGURE 4-4

Twitter lets you enter your location to show your followers where you are based.

With this in mind, do ensure that your Twitter settings reflect a true impression of where you are based by logging into your Twitter account, clicking Settings, and checking out your bio information.

Branding Your Background

A background image is yet another great way to visually express your personal brand. Plan it with your personal brand statement as your guiding light. Although the Twitter background themes are easy to use and may be what you think you need, by using one of the provided images you are branding yourself with the same background as thousands of other Twitter users. The key to creating a great Twitter profile is to set you apart. It's the difference between wearing the same outfit as others and having a suit made especially for you.

By far the easiest way to ensure your profile is unique is to upload your own background image. Simply go to the Settings pane and then click on the Design tab, which will take you to the option to change the background image (see Figure 4-5).

If you are familiar with photo-editing tools such as Adobe Photoshop, you may want to produce something creative that

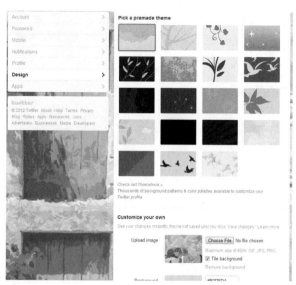

FIGURE 4-5

Twitter's Design pane lets you upload and customize your background image.

immediately familiarizes potential followers with the essence of brand "you." If you don't have the skills for photo editing, you can simply upload a photograph you've taken and play around with the tiled and nontiled options in Twitter (see Figure 4-6) to see what works best aesthetically.

If you want your photo to fill the entire background, the image size and positioning are incredibly important as you don't want to lose your head, so to speak, when the timeline box appears in your profile page. Your image size should be at least 1280 by 1024 pixels. I typically use 1600 by 1200 and even 2048 by 1600 for the background. It's not likely

FIGURE 4-6

The Change Background Image feature lets you experiment with tiled and nontiled options.

that people with huge monitors will stretch their browsers to fill the entire screen, but you never know, so it's best to have a profile that will accommodate all possible viewing arrangements.

Size matters and color counts

You also need to carefully consider file size when creating your background image. Twitter limits the file size to 800K, but I strongly recommend a smaller file size to avoid your background image taking an eternity to load. I prefer to keep the file size under 200K to ensure that loading is never an issue.

Once you've selected your background, you may want to change the colors of the sidebar background and border to complement the overall background image. Don't pick a dark color; otherwise your text may be hard to read. Readability is important to keep in mind as you make your color choices. Your Twitter background can actually work as a virtual business card or brochure if you use the space on the left. You can also use the area at the top to further promote your personal brand message.

FIGURE 4-7

Dean Anthony Gratton (@grattonboy) promotes his personal brand as an author by using a tiled background composed of his published books.

Tiled background tricks

Another option is to locate an image that will work in a tiled effect. Simply search for "tile background" in Google to find thousands of patterns available free or at a low cost. Be sure to adhere to all copyright restrictions and to give credit where credit is due for any work you use as a background tile. If you want to turn one of your own images into a unique background pattern for tiling, there are free tutorials that a quick Google search will take you straight to. Dean Anthony Gratton achieved a great effect by using a tiled image of his books to promote his personal (@grattonboy) brand as a bestselling author and columnist (see Figure 4-7).

Once you have accessed or created the tile selection you want to use as your background image, simply upload it as your Twitter background. Be sure to click the Tile Background option before you save.

Other background options

If your budget allows, by all means use the services of a specialist designer to put together a custom background for your personal brand. Make sure you view the candidate designers' portfolios to ensure that their methodology best suits the look and feel you are seeking. Like everything else in life, each designer has his or her own individual style that may or may not suit you, so take your time in selecting someone who will work in sync with your brand message.

FIGURE 4-8

Tools such as TwitBacks offer a range of free and low-cost background design options.

If, on the other hand, you're restricted by budget but don't want to use one of the Twitter options for your profile background, there's a huge selection of design sites that will provide you with the tools you need to easily create a background on a low-cost or even free basis, depending on the templates your choose. A few of my favorites are Twitrbackgrounds (www.twitrbackgrounds.com), TwitBacks (www.twitbacks.com), shown in Figure 4-8, and Free Twitter Designer (www.freetwitterdesigner.com).

What's Next?

Your killer profile is now armed with the wow factor it needs to attract those all-important followers but, before you step onto the Twitter stage, you need to know how to ensure that your content builds a strong and trusted dialogue for your brand. The next chapter reveals the four types of tweets you need to quickly build your popularity and influence across the Twitterverse.

"Four in wondrous motion."

—*King John*

5

The Four Types of Tweets and Why They Matter

Some people instinctively understood it!

Others imitated it. But it was the instinctual "psychologists" among us who dared to uncover and reveal the secrets of their success. I'm talking about the secrets to creating that perfect stream of daily tweets. The one that attracts numerous followers and keeps them retweeting and coming back for more.

Formatting Comes First

I've gradually come to see social media as a means to create your own personal brand show. A show that people tune into on a daily basis to experience a taste of brand "you." It's a show that you need to fine-tune for it to appeal to as many like minds and associated needs as possible, and it's one whose charm needs to be channeled into a carefully blended mix of content that will delight and engage around the clock. I explain more about this in Chapter 8.

Your Twitter stream's content will, of course, be personal to you and your brand. However, it's the formatting behind the content that I focus on in this chapter. And it's a format that, if adhered to, will make your Twitter account a certain winner with followers.

The SITE formula is an easy one to remember, as Figure 5-1 shows.

So Why Do I Need a Formula, Anyway?

I've already established how important Twitter has become to the personal brand for self-expression and your ability to quickly add and share value. Basically, Twitter is copywriting to the tune of 140 characters or less, which can be an art form to master. Each tweet needs to be constructed with a purpose and brand mission in mind.

FIGURE 5-1

The SITE formula for the four types of tweets that you need to understand

This is where the SITE formula comes in. It's pretty much a fail-safe way of ensuring that your Twitter stream contains the right balance of information, acclaim, and reciprocation.

You need to ensure that each tweet you send works in harmony with the rest of your stream to provide that all-important brand channel. Although the formula won't actually write the tweets for you, it will give you a steadfast foundation on which to plan your Twittertorial calendar, something that I explain in Chapter 7.

Tweeting to the Power of Four

So, it's time to lift the lid on the SITE formula and take you through the four essential types of tweet your need to understand and work with to build your personal brand through Twitter.

Type 1: Share

I've already described how powerful Twitter can be in sourcing and curating information about any subject. Using Twitter's Advanced Search tool (see Figure 5-2) you can find tweets about anything and everything you're interested in.

Search for those topics that best denote your personal brand in terms of what you're trying to promote and resonate through your stream. Search by one or more words that relate to your brand (keywords) or use hashtags (#) to locate any trending topics.

Once you find the tweets, be sure to follow the originator of the source, along with anyone else involved with the tweet and then share it through a retweet, which I like to think of as "Twitter applause," acknowledging the original tweeter by adding the letters "RT" or the word "via" before their Twitter handle and adding your comments or recommendation if space allows. Figure 5-3 shows examples of this type of tweet in action.

FIGURE 5-2

Twitter's Advanced Search feature helps you to locate tweets to share.

FIGURE 5-3

Two examples of how the Share tweet might be used by including the word "via" before the Twitter handle of the original tweeter (top) or by adding the letters "RT" to denote a retweet (bottom).

Type 2: Inform

The Inform tweet introduces new knowledge and content to your Twitter audience. The long-term benefits of this type of tweet are the ones that stamp you as an expert in your field and identify you as a source of value that is definitely worth following. Inform tweets rely on your ability to both create and curate great content. It's also a good idea to link them back to posts on your personal brand blog or website.

Dean Anthony Gratton
@grattonboy

For the latest #wireless industry news and gossip read my monthly Incisor.TV column:
bit.ly/uWXoLn #TeamGratton

FIGURE 5-4

Dean Anthony Gratton (@grattonboy) uses Inform tweets to draw his audience back to his website where he features extracts from his wireless technology column.

FIGURE 5-5

Cordiva Raven uses Twitter to inform her followers about her latest blog posts and to build her reputation as a technology expert.

My husband (@grattonboy) is a great example of this. He uses the Inform tweet to regularly draw his audience to his website (see Figure 5-4), where he features extracts from his latest magazine column and promotions for his latest books. The Inform tweet has not only marked him as a wireless technology expert but has substantially increased traffic to his website and consequently increased sales of his books.

Corvida Raven (@Corvida) built a successful personal brand using Twitter and extended it to her blog SheGeeks (see Figure 5-5), branding the logo with a background print of her Twitter handle to further reinforce its impact. She uses Inform tweets to link her audience back to her blog posts and has clearly made her mark as a technology expert, being listed in *Fast Company* as "an influential woman in technology."

Remember that the Inform tweet *shouldn't* be all about you! This type of tweet is a means of spreading great content to your followers, which means you'll need to hone your curation skills to find those snippets of information, articles, quotes, and images that everyone will want to share. I show you how to achieve this in Chapter 7, where I reveal the secrets of sourcing that go far beyond clever curation, with minimum impact on your precious time.

Type 3: Thank

The third type of tweet is so important and yet it's one that is foolishly overlooked by many.

When someone retweets you, or engages with you in any way, thank them! When someone posts something of particular interest to you, don't just share it — thank them! And when someone new starts following you — the first thing they should receive in return is a personal message of thanks from you.

I'm going to raise a slightly contentious issue now: automated direct messages (DMs). Automated DMs are a method of tweeting that is often frowned upon, but one I believe can't be ignored as your following grows. If you follow the steps laid down in the book, you'll receive hundreds of new followers each week (or maybe each day), which will make sending a message of thanks to each individual an impossible task. That's why, in Part Four, I show you the tools available to keep those messages personal without eating up your precious time.

A thank-you is a very powerful type of tweet and is one that will get you remembered and help to build your personal brand loyalty.

FIGURE 5-6

The @Connect feature in Twitter lets you see both your mentions and interactions.

FIGURE 5-7

Thanking multiple people in a single tweet

As your following builds, don't let your manners slip. Twitter lets you check all the tweets that mention you in its @Connect feature on your profile page by going to either the Mentions or Interactions pane (see Figure 5-6).

Once you see who has mentioned you, depending on the scenario and timing, you might thank them with a public message, such as: "Thanks so much @ellies58 for the great mention ☺"

If you are thanking someone for a retweet, remember to include the original tweet or link if possible. You can also include a hashtag, such as, "Thank you for the #teamgratton retweets!"

By using the hashtag (#teamgratton, in this case), your audience can identify other relevant people they may want to follow.

Alternatively, you can thank multiple followers at once, as shown in Figure 5-7.

Or, you may decide just to send a direct message by beginning the tweet with a "d" and removing the @ before the Twitter handle. You can only send a direct message if the person you want to thank is following you. For example: "d ellies58 You are so sweet to think of me! Thank you for tweeting such a great post – I'll certainly RT!"

Some thank-you exceptions

There are certain scenarios where recognizing users for sharing your content is unnecessary or impractical:

▸ Ignore Twitter bot retweets because there's no human relationship to build. I tell you more about how to identify bots — automated tweeters — in Chapter 6.

▸ Beware of retweets by "get rich quick" and multilevel marketing (MLM) tweets. The primary objective of these tweets is to grow followers. Show thanks for these at your own peril, as initiating conversation with the people behind them will probably result in a flood of their MLM friends also following your account, which can make it difficult to locate and follow your genuine followers.

▸ If someone retweets you several times in one day, be selective in how you thank him or her. It's not necessary to match tweet for tweet in your thank-you process. A single "thanks for all your RTs today" is usually sufficient.

How not to use the Thank type of tweet

1. Do not post numerous thank you tweets back to back. It makes your profile timeline non-value-added for new prospective followers viewing your profile. Twitter features the three most recent tweets in the user profile preview pane (shown in Figure 5-8), so consider two your maximum number for consecutive thank-you retweets at any given time.

2. Avoid posting thank-you retweets during peak content retweet hours. Instead, target off-peak Twitter times so as not to bore your following.

3. Do not send a direct message that merely says, "Thanks for the RT!" This type of tweet has no conversational value and equates to

FIGURE 5-8

Clicking on a user profile in Twitter opens a preview pane revealing the last three tweets sent from that account. It also shows whether the user is following you and gives you the option to follow or unfollow.

spam. Personalize the message so it adds value or ignites conversation.

4. Remember to be consistent in your public thanks and don't restrict them to a select few. Use direct messages for occasional individual thanks as needed and set aside time to engage and thank your audience, remembering to include the original link or tweet in any thanks retweet.

Type 4. Engage

The Engage type of tweet does just that for both your stream of content and your following.

By sourcing and curating information pertaining to tweets and followers of interest, you can expand on their Inform tweets with complementary comments and links. An Engage tweet is also a great way of building a conversation within your community of followers.

For example, you can introduce a question or scenario that you need your followers to expand on with their thoughts and ideas. You can even use tools and applications such as Twitter Polls (www.polls.tw), shown in Figure 5-9, to create a community buzz as Corvida Raven (@corvida) did with her slightly controversial Twitter sex poll, shown in Figure 5-10.

Engaging your audience means doing far more than just following them. The Engage tweet means asking questions, seeking advice, and joining discussions. It's a close kin to the Share tweet, where you'll reply to interesting people and add comments to your retweets.

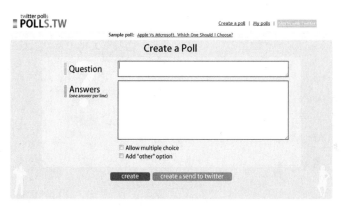

FIGURE 5-9

Using an application such as Twitter Polls to post your Engage tweets can quickly build a buzz among your followers.

FIGURE 5-10

Corvida Raven (@corvida) initiated a controversial Twitter Poll to grab her followers' attention and engage them in the conversation.

FIGURE 5-11

The #Discover feature on Twitter is intuitive to your interests, location, and language. It becomes more intelligent the more you use it.

The Engage tweet lets other Twitter users know that you care about what they have to say. It shows that you are knowledgeable in your industry and presents you as a valuable Twitter user.

Some of the most effective forms of Engage tweet use current trending topics or hashtags to engage others. These both offer a great way to immediately jump into a conversation that already has many voices involved. Find the trending topics and hashtags that best suit your brand message by using the Twitter search tools or try out the intuitive Twitter #Discover feature (see Figure 5-11), which finds stories and other trending content based on your interests, connections, location, and language.

Find the content that excites you the most and jump right in!

The four types of tweet that make up the SITE formula are your foundation to Twitter success. By using the formula on a daily basis with your Twittertorial calendar, which I show you how to build in Chapter 7, you'll have all the tools and knowledge you need to make your personal brand on Twitter a sure-fire success.

"What are you? Your name, your quality?
And why did you answer this present summons?"

—*King Lear*

6

Building Your Followers: Quality Versus Quantity

When building your following, it's hard not to let a little thing like numbers get in the way of your decision-making. Everyone wants to be the most popular person in the playground, and Twitter is just another such playground.

But here's where we need to put our professional heads on and consider what we want to actually gain from the platform in terms of potential revenue. Yes, I've said it before and I'm saying it again: I firmly believe that it is possible to make money as a result of the connections and relationships built via Twitter. The quality-versus-quantity conundrum is the issue that surrounds its probability.

I'm Listening! Or Am I?

Numbers alone don't equate to followers in the true sense of the word and, as I've explained, emotions govern our decision-making processes. There are thousands of bots that follow you indiscriminately on Twitter without the least bit of interest in you or your brand, Although this increased following might

initially be a great ego booster, it's a hollow victory in terms of your brand message having any real impact.

Imagine you're the host of a show on your favorite radio station. Every day you go on air with lively, witty, and challenging content. Your show features promotional content that you want your listeners to emotionally connect with and, over time, invest in. So you need to ensure that your listeners are actually listening. Your listening figures are tremendous and you experience that flush of power-driven delight that comes from the knowledge that your show is hugely popular and influential. But, on closer inspection of the listening figures, you learn that only 10 percent of your listeners actually listen to your show each day and that, out of those 10 percent, only 2 percent call in or invest in your promotions. The others may have tuned into your channel, but they are neither listening nor responding.

The autofollow bots on Twitter are a lot like these superfluous listeners. They look out for keywords and follow without the least bit of interest in your brand, other than to latch onto it as a sounding board for the automated spam tweets and messages that do nothing to boost your Twitter appeal or the content of your stream. The bots are there for one purpose and one purpose only: to launch a full-scale attack with a barrage of spam polluted links.

But how do you find them and, more important, what can you do about them?

How to Become a Botinator

I've developed my own anti-bot checklist to keep my Twitter timeline free from Twitter spammers and the dreaded bots. I like to think of myself as a kind of bot Terminator — or Botinator — and here's my strategy for being one:

1. They'll be back!

First, I always wait a few days before following back, which gives me an opportunity to manually vet any new followers before making a decision.

It also gives me a chance to see whether they are using one of the most common tricks of automated Twitter bots, which is to follow someone purely to see if they follow back. This is fine in itself, but the difference between real people and software is that bots put you on a

FIGURE 6-1

A stream of junk or spam tweets with no other interaction is a clear indication of a bot follower.

timer and unfollow you after a certain period of time, only to follow you again a few days later to send you another junk tweet.

If you *still* don't follow back, the automated software will continue until you either follow back or block the user. Waiting a few days before you check out someone's profile gives you the opportunity to peruse their Twitter stream before committing to follow. If you see a stream of junk or spam-related links with no other interaction (see Figure 6-1) or a chain of follow and unfollow behavior, it's most likely the work of a bot and is best ignored.

2. Same script, different cast

Look for the giveaway scenario, where thoughts of *déjà vu* appear and you realize that you've read this tweet somewhere before. Bots like to take different Twitter handles to push out the same content time and time again, as shown in Figure 6-2. Make a note of the tweets you believe are particularly suspicious and look for reoccurrences from new followers. Also bear in mind that many genuine Twitter followers have their accounts hijacked by bots on a regular basis. This hijacking occurs when they subscribe to a Twitter service or third-party application, where Twitter account information needs to be entered. Always ensure that you sign up to only those applications you know are safe.

3. Invasion of the profile pic snatchers

Remember that they clone! Spammers and bots like to use the same profile picture for hundreds of accounts, which are often (and I say this without any sexism intended) images of scantily clad, attractive young women (see Figure 6-3).

FIGURE 6-2

Bots like to use different Twitter handles to post the same spam messages.

FIGURE 6-3

Bots often sign up to several Twitter accounts using the same profile picture.

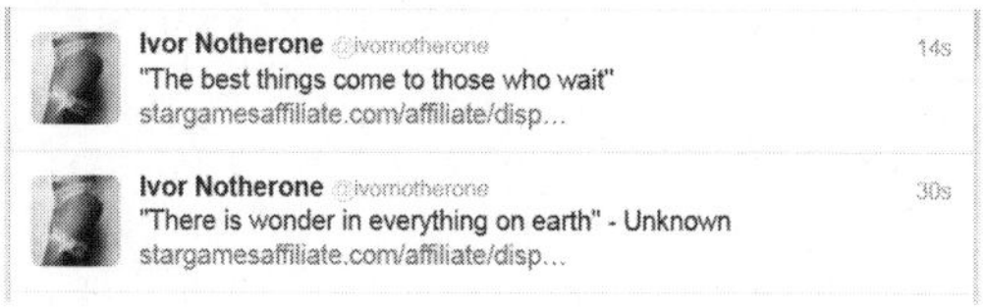

Ivor Notherone @ivornotherone   14s
"The best things come to those who wait"
stargamesaffiliate.com/affiliate/disp...

Ivor Notherone @ivornotherone   30s
"There is wonder in everything on earth" - Unknown
stargamesaffiliate.com/affiliate/disp...

FIGURE 6-4

Bots often use quotes to attract followers to click on their affiliate and sales page links.

I've been followed by multiple bots using the same profile photo dozens of times on the same day and for some reason they think I won't notice. If you spot a profile picture that looks familiar, you've more than likely seen it before — and it's probably a bot!

4. Can I compare thee to a summer's bot?

I'm a great lover of quotes, especially the ones that motivate and inspire. I enjoy tweeting the ones that really grab my attention, as do many of my followers. However, this gem of knowledge hasn't escaped the bots' attention and the quote/link strategy is one that many bots choose to adopt to provide the look of an authentic Twitter profile.

So how do you sort the wheat from the chaff? The answer lies in the addition of those affiliate and sales page links they attach to the quotes they tweet (see Figure 6-4). So, if you see a profile with an overabundance of quotes, take a closer look. If these kinds of links are continually attached, they're likely to be the work of a bot, using the charm offensive as link bait.

TrueTwit Validation

TrueTwit markets itself as the validation service for Twitter. It was created to help its users sift through their followers, letting them separate the humans from the bots.

That's all well and good, but it turns out that TrueTwit is a double-edged sword. It works by sending your new followers an automated direct message (DM) asking them to validate whether they are a bot or spammer by completing a CAPTCHA (Completely Automated Public Turing Test to Tell Computers and Humans Apart). The validation involves asking them to complete a simple test (see Figure 6-5) that is easy for a

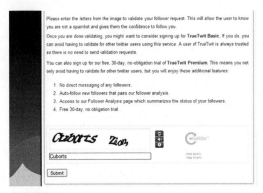

FIGURE 6-5

TrueTwit validation asks you to complete a CAPTCHA to prove you're neither a spammer nor a bot.

human but difficult for a computer, such as entering numbers and letters displayed as distorted graphics. If TrueTwit receives a correct answer to the CAPTCHA, it is assumed to have been entered by a person and is validated.

But just because someone is able to pass the CAPTCHA validation test doesn't mean he or she isn't a spammer. Passing the test merely indicates a real person rather than a bot, but he or she may still be posting "click here" links all day long, which makes the person no better than a bot in what he or she adds to your Twitter stream.

Another problem is the TrueTwit validation itself. If some of your followers also follow many people, it can be difficult for them to keep up with all the DM requests asking for validation. Failure to respond may, of course, mean the account is a bot, but it could also mean that the person receiving the DM is too overwhelmed to deal with the request or that he or she just didn't see the message.

Many people see the TrueTwit validation process as an inconvenience and often choose to ignore the requests, so bear in mind that you could be losing valuable and loyal followers by subscribing to the application (see Figure 6-6).

In fact, the only way to avoid receiving a TrueTwit validation request via DM is to register with TrueTwit, which can almost come across as a threatening "sign up with us or else" message, again defeating the intention of the service to help clean up Twitter.

FIGURE 6-6

Not everyone likes using TrueTwit, and it can actually be detrimental to attracting quality followers.

The Perfect Balance

It's easy to quip that quality is always better than quantity, but quality by itself doesn't mean much on Twitter unless it comes in bulk. So why look at quality versus quantity at all? Why not instead focus on quality *plus* quantity? After all, you ultimately need to achieve both to get the most out of Twitter for your personal brand.

There's a method of balancing the quality *and* the quantity of your followers and your tweets on Twitter that I've perfected over the years and want to share with you now:

1. Find your Twitter birds of a feather

Seek out people who are using Twitter for the same reasons you are using it. For example, if you're a designer, photographer, writer, or musician, then follow those people with the same interests as yours, like other musicians, writers, and so on. That's *quality*.

You can use the @Connect feature on Twitter to search for like-minded people. You also can use one or more of the many Twitter directories, such as Twellow (see Figure 6-7), Just Tweet It, and TweetFind. This exercise will not only help gain more followers (that's *quantity*), but it will also provide you with followers more willing to converse, retweet, and share your tweets with others due to your shared common interests (that's *quality* again).

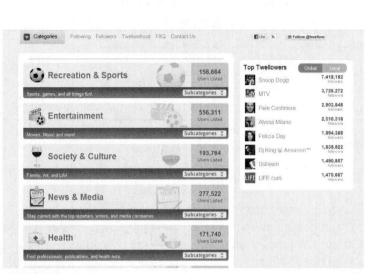

FIGURE 6-7

Twellow is the Twitter equivalent of the Yellow Pages. It's free to register your account and is a useful base to find followers with the same interests as you.

2. Base your following strategy on the SITE formula

I introduced the four types of tweets (Share, Inform, Thank, and Exchange) via the SITE formula in Chapter 5, and here's where the tweets become even more useful. Not only does this method of tweeting make your brand stand out, it's also an incredibly useful gauge for measuring the *quality* of other potential followers. Take a look at the Twitter streams of any new followers and see whether they are using the four types of tweet or whether they are just blanket posting with no real purpose or interest in others. This exercise will provide you with an immediate impression of their value.

3. Host a tweetup

A tweetup is a small, casual event where you invite your Twitter followers to get together on an informal basis, while sharing the event on Twitter. A tweetup helps you put a face to a name, *building a stronger bond*

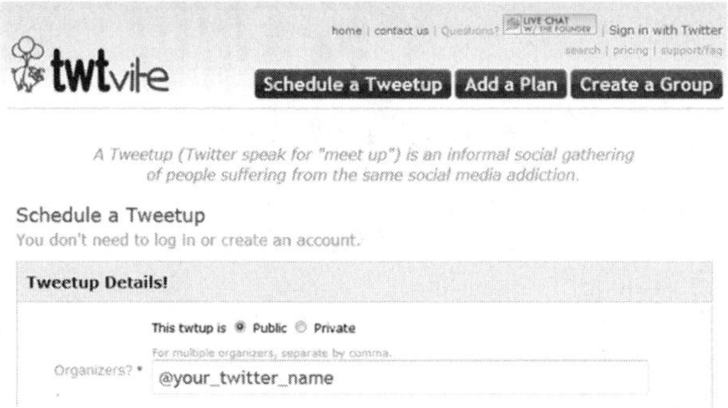

FIGURE 6-8

Services like Twtvite can help you to easily organize a tweetup.

with that person. You will also gather other followers who are likely to bring their Twitter friends along to the tweetup.

Your tweetup can be as simple as asking your followers if they would like to meet for a drink or dinner. You can meet at a coffeehouse, bar, or even someone's house. A tweetup also works if you are traveling and have a lot of followers in a particular area.

If you want to be more formal and attract more people, create a hashtag for the event and an invitation page. A service like Twtvite, shown in Figure 6-8, can help you set up your first tweetup quickly and easily.

A Perfect Union for Your Personal Brand

By now the union between quality and quantity should be clear. The advice in this chapter will let you harness both attributes to ensure that your personal brand has a strong following that is truly worth its weight in gold.

The next two chapters reveal how to put together your ultimate Twittertorial calendar and how to translate it into your own 24-hour online brand show.

"Look in the Calendar and bring me word."

—*Julius Caesar*

7

Creating Your Twittertorial Calendar

One of the main gripes voiced about shifting to a social-media-centric way of promotion is the amount of hours we see each of the various platforms eating into our precious time. That's why flexible scheduling is so important. I say "flexible" because there's only so much content, or *foundation tweets* as I call them, that you can use at a later date without things changing and removing its value.

Creating content that is particularly relevant to your followers at that very moment has disproportionately high benefits. Being on-trend not only gives you structure (relieving you from the "what should I write about next?" dilemma) but also increases the likelihood that people will interact with your content, that it will be retweeted, and that it will warrant an eventual call to action in terms of revenue possibilities.

It's All in the Planning

When I first started building my personal brand on Twitter, I did so in a "fly by the seat of my pants," ad-hoc fashion. As my following started to substantially grow, however, it became more and more difficult to manage the time and flow of my content. I realized there had to be a more efficient way of managing my content stream, so I looked to traditional methods of planning to build my formula on.

My mind wandered back to my days at *News International* in England, where our editorial calendars were our bibles, and a "Eureka!" moment occurred. Surely I could adopt the same principles of content management and transfer them to my social media platforms to bring much needed structure to my content stream.

I realized that the goal of reflecting what is current and relevant to my audience was something of an art form, but by linking to trusted curation sources (which I explain later in this chapter), you can master the art of great Twitter content and set it down in calendar form.

This realization came to me prior to defining the four types of tweets, which I introduced in Chapter 5. In fact, putting together my Twitter-centered editorial calendar — or my Twittertorial calendar as I now like to call it — helped me realize how different types of tweets could work in synergy to effectively promote a brand message.

Planning your Twittertorial calendar in advance takes courage. To begin with, it can feel a little like stumbling around in the dark. You're not entirely sure what you can reach out and grab onto for support along the way, and the ground below can seem unsteady. Again, this is where the power of your personal brand statement will play a huge part in helping you plot your course.

Mastering the Art of Clever Curation

Make no mistake, clever curation is indeed an art form that starts with a clear understanding of your personal brand statement, which I introduced in Chapter 3. You need to fully comprehend all it stands for and all that you, as a personal brand, want to achieve from its message. It's a case of mentally dissecting your brand into clearly definable and highly searchable keywords and phrases that will lay the foundation for your curation framework.

Using my @grattongirl brand as an example, my personal brand statement reads, "I delight in helping others create and unleash their personal brand on Twitter."

I can break the keywords down to "help," "create," and "branding" and then build on these words to find searchable keyword alternatives such as:

 ▶ Help = assist, support, guide, teach, show, explain
 ▶ Create = build, produce, craft, make
 ▶ Branding = Imprinting, stamping, marking

I can then break my statement down into searchable phrases such as "I delight in helping others create and unleash their personal brand on Twitter":

 ▶ Creating a personal brand
 ▶ Building a personal brand
 ▶ Unleashing your personal brand

Or "I delight in helping others create and unleash their personal brand on Twitter":

▶ The joy in helping others
▶ The joy of giving
▶ Motivational support

Or "I delight in helping others create and unleash their personal brand on Twitter":

▶ Twitter help
▶ Using Twitter creatively
▶ Creating your brand on Twitter

And there are dozens more combinations I can draw on to find the most brand-relevant content for my followers.

Next, I use my keywords and phrases to find fresh and relevant content on my search engine sites and other great curation resources such as StumbleUpon (see Figure 7-1). This content will make up my Inform tweets, which I introduced in Chapter 5.

Be sure to check the dates of any sites you search for on Google using its Search Tools option in the bottom left of the Google website to make sure they contain current information (see Figure 7-2). Be sure to

FIGURE 7-1

StumbleUpon is a great curation tool for locating new content based on your keywords.

Any time
Past hour
Past 24 hours
Past week
Past month
Past year
Custom range...
From:
To:
ex. 23/9/2004
Search

All results
Sites with images
Related searches
Visited pages
Not yet visited
Dictionary
Reading level
Social
Translated foreign pages
Verbatim

Fewer search tools

FIGURE 7-2

Google's Search Tools feature makes it easy to customize your search and locate the latest content to keep your tweets fresh and relevant.

also check the dates of any content found on StumbleUpon to keep your links as up to date as possible.

Once you've curated a great range of content that fits well with your personal brand, save a brief summary of each proposed tweet with a link to the URL where the content can be found. I place mine in a separate folder on my computer so I know where to easily find them. My folder is labeled Curation and is broken into subfolders determined by my keywords to make my curated content easier to locate when I put together my calendar (see Figure 7-3).

FIGURE 7-3

Organize your curation in a main folder containing sub-folders based on your personal brand keyword findings.

FIGURE 7-4

Some example brand anchor tweets, enticing followers to check out (and with any luck purchase) this book

Creating Your Brand Anchors

Having curated a great range of content for your brand from other sources on the web, the next step is to compile links to every article, post, infographic, quote, and other related item that is either written by or attributed directly to you. I call these your *brand anchors*, as they are fundamentally routed in brand "you."

Once you've put together your brand anchors, it's time to get creative with your proposed tweets to draw your audience to them. For example, the links to my books are great brand anchors and I have found a variety of ways to direct my followers to their online order pages using creative tweeting, as shown below in Figures 7-4.

Using Key Events

All good curators draw on key events throughout the year to source new content that best showcases their brand message. Start by looking at future events that have a personal connection to brand "you." A florist, for example, would pay particular attention to Mother's Day and Valentine's Day and mark them as key occasions in his or her Twittertorial calendar. A technology consultant would probably include SXSW and CeBIT in his or her lists. As you create your list, make sure that every event has a date associated with it for your calendar.

Order the list by date, and begin by focusing on the events occurring in the next three months. Also pay particular attention to the biggest events in your year ahead and those where you are speaking or contributing in some way. In fact, try to find as many ways of associating your brand with these events to turn them from curated links to brand anchors that showcase brand "you"!

A Little More Courage

Don't be afraid to let your imagination run away in this process. Think of different takes on how you present your content. For example, if you're planning to cover a local industry event, why not start a tweetup among the attendees, with a specific hashtag (I explain more about this in Chapter 10) to bring a sense of community to both the event and to your followers, who can then also participate via your united tweets. A tweetup, as I introduced in Chapter 6, is basically a means of forming a Twitter group at a get-together, which is then tweeted out to each of the attendee's followers. It's a great way of bringing like-minded tweeters together and building on your following at the same time. You can use your Twittertorial calendar to both initiate and promote the tweetup and, of course, to follow up on it after the event.

If you're aware that relevant industry data is going to be published, plan ahead and have a template ready to create a unique infographic of it, which you can tweet to your followers.

If you're aware that a competitor is about to announce a new product or service, don't be afraid to steal its limelight by tweeting something to distract attention from it, whether it be a new report that leads opinion in a different direction or news of something equally big from your side of the trenches. For example, I don't think it's a coincidence that Microsoft allegedly tried to generate buzz by revealing the new Windows 8 logo on the same day that Apple's OS X Mountain Lion was announced.

Your Content List

The following is an exaggerated example list of what you might now have to work with based on a huge amount of personal interests. Not everyone will have a range as wide as this and, as previously mentioned, it's good to hone your list into a personal, brand-specific niche. But I hope it will give you an idea of how your list could look at this stage:

- **Your brand anchors**, including blog post links, other article links, your product or service links, other links relating to you (press releases, citations, and mentions), and personal insight links (photos, quotes, and memories that have emotional value).
- **Your industry/niche's Inform tweets**, including industry news and events, local events and tweetups, annual reports and research reports, industry awards, industry conferences (especially those you will attend or at which you are speaking), industry exhibitions (especially those you will attend or at which you exhibit), partner events, new product/service/industry launches in your arena, product/service upgrades and relaunches, announcements about big new clients, and competitors
- **Occasions**, including niche events and celebrations (for example, Crufts for dog lovers and planting season for gardeners), widely recognized events (for example, National Book Month), and events just made up for PR (for example, National Taco Week)
- **Politics and community topics**, including local/regional/national election cycles, new laws and bills, openings and closing of political seasons, and annual budget announcement
- **Holidays and celebrations**, including public holidays, bank and federal holidays, other national holidays, things that everyone celebrates (such as major sports championships or end of the school year), unofficial holidays (such as Valentine's Day, Halloween, Mother's Day, Father's Day, April Fool's Day, Friday the 13th, February 29th, and Pi Day), holidays from other cultures, the first day of spring/summer/fall/winter, the equinoxes and solstices, the start and end of daylight savings time, and the tax season
- **Humorous quotes relating to your interests**
- **Photography that tells a story relating to brand "you."**
- **Events**, such as historical events (such as the Battle of Hastings, 9/11, Bloody Sunday, D-Day, Columbus's landing in the Americas, the fall of the Berlin Wall, and the Ides of March), celebrity birthdays/marriages/deaths, science/technology events (for example, the first moon landing and the first World's Fair), tragic events (such as natural disasters and plane crashes), once-in-a-

lifetime events (such as Halley's Comet, the last NASA space shuttle launch, the royal wedding/coronation, a solar eclipse, the turn of a century), and independence days

▶ **Sporting events**, including annual sports events (such as the Super Bowl, FA Cup Final, varsity rugby, and local boat race), annual sporting seasons (such as the NFL playoffs, the Six Nations, and March Madness), periodic sporting events (such as the Ryder Cup, Olympics, Commonwealth Games, Ashes, UEFA Championship, and Cricket World Cup)

▶ **TV, film, and stage**, including the first episode and final episode or new season of popular TV shows, TV scheduling seasons (for example, the fall TV schedule), big movie releases, new stage shows (such as theatrical plays, musicals, ballet, and opera), and awards shows (such as the Oscars, BAFTAs, Emmys, and Tonys)

▶ **Music**, including big album/single releases, chart announcements (for example, Christmas Number 1 and Festive Fifty), artists on tour, festivals (such as Coachella, Glastonbury, Burning Man, and Latitude), and awards shows (such as the Grammys, Country Music Awards, and *British idol*)

▶ **Shopping and products**, including anticipated new product releases (such as new tablets and the latest model cars), video game releases, limited-availability products (such as Girl Scout Cookies and Cadbury's Creme Eggs), new store openings, and shopping events (such as the spring sale season, Black Friday, and Back to School)

▶ **Publishing**, including book series installments (such as the latest *Twilight* novel), big magazine events (such as the *Economist's The World in 2012* and *Sports Illustrated's* swimsuit edition)

Putting It All Together

So now you have all the pieces to your puzzle. But bear in mind that the list itself is far from definitive. The key now is to put its items together in a way that paints a clear picture of your brand.

You can use your list of curated content to create your *foundation tweets*. These are the tweets that stay in your calendar and can be planned and positioned well in advance.

FIGURE 7-5

An example of how the foundation tweets in a Twittertorial calendar might look

You can also use your keywords and phrases to add *suggestion tweets* to the calendar. These are tweets that need to contain freshly curated content to keep them current.

Whatever month you choose as the first month to start tweeting from your Twittertorial calendar is Month 1. Let's say you're starting to plan your Twittertorial calendar in September to begin using in October. In this case, October is Month 1, November is Month 2 and so on. You'll need to incorporate your four types of tweets in your calendar's construction, so the first day of Month 1 might look like the one in Figure 7-5.

Day 1 shows my brand anchor tweets for the day in blue. These are also foundation tweets, accessible from my folders and personal links and are unlikely to need amending. The other tweets are suggestion tweets that point the way for me to curate great content for the day.

Notice that I don't include any Thank or Engage tweet notifications. These are necessary but reactionary tweets that can occur at different times each day and are wholly dependent on follower behavior and content, making calendar placement impossible.

Also notice that, at this stage, I haven't allocated specific times for the tweets to go out but have merely planned the content I want to provide for my followers. I explain more about why this is the case in the next two chapters.

What you need to do now is to turn your Twittertorial calendar into your own unique brand show. So, what are you waiting for?

"All the world's a stage,
and all the men and women merely players."

—*As You Like It*

8

Your Brand, Your Show

My parents often reminisced fondly about their childhood family gatherings around the fireplace on a Sunday evening. Glasses of warm milk in their hands and their tummies still full from lunchtime's Sunday roast, as their parents tuned-in to the early evening's line-up of entertainment on the radio.

The popular shows of the time included Abbott and Costello, Burns and Allen, *Easy Aces*, and *Ethel and Albert* in the United States, and *The Goon Show* and Hancock's Half Hour across the pond in England, where my parents both grew up.

"There was something special about the radio. Something about the listening," my father told me. "It allowed us to use our imaginations to paint pictures. Television has deprived us of that gift."

From the White House to the Moon

But the times they were a-changing, and the counterculture of the 1960s and 1970s saw the rapid invasion of a new form of media through the evolution of television networks and the types of program they were starting to present. By the turn of the swinging '60s, television sets were becoming a commonplace addition in the home, and exciting new changes began taking place in program content and production techniques.

Millions of people were able to watch Martin Luther King, Jr.'s "I Have a Dream" speech, broadcast live in 1963 (see Figure 8-1), which marked a shift in the political use of television as a means of drawing the public's attention to campaigns and causes. By the end of the '60s, the dream reached lunar proportions as we gathered in front of our boxes to watch the first man walk on the moon. As children, we sang along with Big Bird and decorated our Christmas trees to the Muppets' *Christmas Carol*.

A Shift in Power

Then came the 1980s with the arrival of the video recorder, and suddenly the game changed yet again. Our media choices were extended, as we were no longer restricted to watching the clock to catch our favorite shows. Now we could record, rewind, fast-forward, and even watch our favorite clips in slow motion. We were empowered by a new ability to watch what we wanted when we wanted. Video stores opened in the thousands, where we could rent movies to share with friends and family at a time governed by us and us alone. Suddenly, the viewer was in control — and there was no going back!

The Incredible Shrinking Attention Span

This shift in power was intoxicating, but it also began a psychological shift in how we chose to deal with the growing number of media choices on offer. As the options slowly increased, our attention spans began to shrink.

Today, we require our education and entertainment, or *edutainment* as it's recently been termed, in chunks. They need to grab our attention immediately to keep us hanging around.

And that's not just my opinion. A 2011 study by research group Visible Measures found that, after watching an online video for just 60 seconds, 44.1 percent of viewers would have clicked away.

This phenomenon, known as *viewer abandonment*, is of intense interest to those who make today's media or advertise in it. Visible Measures studied the abandonment rate of 40 million online videos over 7 billion viewings, as shown in Figure 8-1. Music videos had especially high rates of abandonment, as did videos slow to reach a punch-line. For example, a Budweiser video about a man humiliated while buying pornography lost almost 40 percent of viewers in the first 10 seconds.

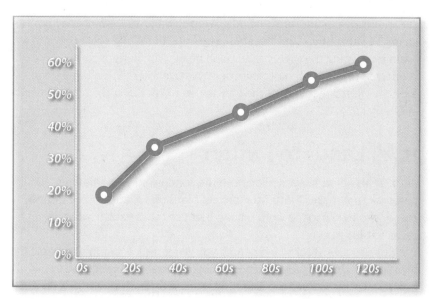

FIGURE 8-1

A 2011 study by Visible Measures shows the viewer abandonment rates and number of seconds until abandonment of 40 million videos over 7 billion viewings.

From a Set-Top Box to a Streaming World

We live in a world today where we can access information, entertainment, and education almost anywhere, whether traveling on a bus downtown, strolling in the park, or passing time at the airport. We carry our content with us and it's become pocket-size! We can flit between taking a call, writing an email, reading a text, and watching our favorite band play live on stage at Radio City Music Hall. With all these choices constantly available to us, it's no wonder that our synapses have adapted to filter out any unwanted noise.

This need to filter our choices has led to another huge shift. According to the Associated Press, hundreds of thousands of viewers are ditching their monthly cable or satellite TV service in favor of streaming video. The AP examined cable and satellite companies' quarterly returns and concluded that they had lost about 195,000 subscribers in the second quarter of 2011.

Interestingly, the study included Verizon and AT&T, which may be losing TV subscribers, but are equally gaining in mobile subscribers, again reinforcing the theory that we all need to be permanently connected to the content we choose to receive today. It reaffirms Dean Anthony Gratton's theory of the Lawnmower Man Effect that I introduced in Chapter 2.

It All Leads to Twitter

It's this sense of immediacy and the condensed edutainment potential that makes Twitter the perfect platform to launch your online brand "show." (I use the word "show" because that's exactly what it's going to be!)

So, let's take stock of everything you've learned so far in this book. By now you have gained a strong sense of your personal brand, you know how to identify and use the four types of tweets, and you are well on your way to building a great Twittertorial calendar.

Now, you're going to use all these elements to transform your Twitter stream into your personal online show. A dazzling content feed that will keep your audience both entertained and educated, while it works around the clock to showcase brand "you"!

Building Your Brand from the Foundation Up

Your Twittertorial calendar already contains your foundation tweets (see Chapter 7), so let's start with them. They might be quotes or links having edutainment value. Your first foundation tweet of the day marks the way forward for all the other types of tweet you need to insert to create your show. You should incorporate the four types of tweets in your stream that I introduced in Chapter 5 and ensure that your suggestion tweets (see Chapter 7) are curated with the most relevant content.

Mixing It Up

Where possible, and especially in the early days of building your brand on Twitter, try to keep to content that is related or specific to your field. But, just because your field is technical or maybe rooted in finance or industry, that doesn't mean your tweets can't be uplifting and even humorous at times. Remember that you're using Twitter to set yourself apart by emotionally connecting with your followers, so choose a mix of content that will do just that.

Quotations

These are great show-fillers and can be planned in advance as foundation tweets. Many people search specifically for the hashtag #quote to find those gems worth retweeting each day, so ensure that the ones you pick best reflect your brand message.

Bear in mind that the quotes you choose don't necessarily have to spell out your given field but can be relevant through their association with the passion you feel for them. For example, a sports coach might choose to tweet quotes such as "You can out-distance that which is running after you, but not what is running inside you. —Rwandan proverb" #quote #sports" or "I never had a policy; I have just tried to do my very best each and every day. —Abraham Lincoln" #quote #sports"

Both are relative in emotional association, in contrast to "The fewer rules a coach has, the fewer rules there are for players to break. —John Madden" #quote #sports" or "The breakfast of champions is not cereal, it's the opposition. —Nick Seitz #quote #sports"

These are both sports-industry-specific and, therefore, also relevant.

Notice how I've incorporated the hashtags #quote and #sports at the end of each quotation tweet. This addition provides a further search tool for your audience and potential followers. I explain more about the power of hashtags in Chapter 10.

Bread, butter, and conversation

The tweets that include links to brand-related, dynamic articles, and posts are the bread and butter of your daily Twitter show and are what gives it substance and sticking power. I've already introduced some of the curation tools that can be used to locate your articles and posts for scheduling in your show and expand on these further in Part Four. Ultimately, you're looking for posts that follow a particular theme, governed by a variety of factors such as time of year, upcoming events, or a leading item of news.

FIGURE 8-2

Use the here and now to build unique current content for your audience.

Your posts should, of course, include a healthy smattering of your own writing; those tweets I introduced in Chapter 7 as your brand anchors, supplemented by influential posts and articles from trusted sources.

You should also use the here and now to build unique, current content for your audience that's engaging and entices a conversation. For example, a news story you've just heard on the radio or a song that you can't get out of your head. Can you tie them into your brand message in some way?

Even if the connection is abstract, you can use it to start a conversation with your audience. For example, I woke up with the song "Price Tag" by Jessie J in my head a few weeks ago and the lyrics just wouldn't leave me as I tried to write that day. I incorporated my frustration as a tweet in my show (see Figure 8-2). This resulted in numerous retweets and replies from followers, some who found the association humorous and others who had similar stories of irony to tell.

A picture paints a thousand tweets

Include photos, illustrations, infographics, and other images into your show on a daily basis to lift it to another, more exiting dimension. To add cohesion, find a way to keep a regular theme running through that occurs at the same time each day.

As someone who builds brands on Twitter, I try to find pictorial ways to humorously link the platform to everyday situations in life such as sleeping where, on one occasion, I posted a photograph of the perfect Twitter bed (see Figure 8-3).

Photography can also be used to add drama and depth to a tweet as shown in Figure 8-4. These make the tweets more memorable, and a good image is likely to be retweeted many times. Always be sure to give credit where credit's due by including the image copyright and the originator's Twitter handle if appropriate, which is another way of expanding on your quality connections.

FIGURE 8-3

I like to incorporate amusing but brand-relevant photos to provide humor for my audience.

FIGURE 8-4

An example of how photography can be used to add drama to a tweeted statement or quotation

Incorporating great video content

Supporting your brand message through great content includes extending it to video. If you have your own YouTube (or similar) channel relating to your brand, you're off to a flying start and can tweet links to its videos on a regular — perhaps daily — basis, depending on how extensive your library of content is. If you don't yet have a YouTube channel for your brand, start an account and use it to source related video links that will translate into great tweeted content for your show.

As I mentioned earlier in this chapter, the media choices have grown exponentially from year to year and, as a result, our attention spans have shrunk dramatically. Bear this in mind when you choose video content for your brand show and keep the video to 120 seconds or less to avoid the

FIGURE 8-5

TNT's clever YouTube video had stickiness and quickly went viral.

high levels of viewer abandonment I described earlier. Use your judgment in selecting the videos with the most sticking power and those that are likely to go viral.

Don't be afraid to retweet the videos everyone is talking about. They may not be your discovery, but they are the ones your followers will applaud you for including, and that they will be happy to watch and retweet again and again.

A great example of this is the recent Belgium-based TNT promo video, which quickly became viral on YouTube thanks to the thousands of overnight views it received and the way it spread like wildfire on Twitter. The secret of its stickiness is that you need to keep watching to see what happens next! It's a hidden-camera-based promotion where a huge button was placed in a quiet square in a Belgium town with a sign hanging over it reading "Push to add drama" (see Figure 8-5). It goes without saying that, before long, someone did indeed push the button and found themselves surrounded by many acted-out scenes from various movies and drama series. The promotion was only a couple of minutes long, just perfect in terms of keeping viewer attention and creating maximum impact for the TNT brand.

Planning Your Production Schedule

Take a look at Table 8-1 for an example of how I constructed a day's personal brand-show content on Twitter. Each daily show is split into three four-hour blocks: Part 1, Part 2, and Part 3 (see the Schedule column) that I then repeated later in the day for reasons that I explain later in this chapter.

Using your Twittertorial calendar and your curation folders as a base for your schedule means that you've already done much of the work. The remainder should take no more than 60 to 90 minutes a day to complete, although you will need to set aside several hours a day for engaging with your followers through retweets, acknowledgements, replies, and thanks.

I also like to include random, off-the-cuff tweets, such as photographs I've taken at a particular time of day that my followers can relate to, or funny news items that have caught my attention. I occasionally invite my followers to take part in a caption competition, where I provide a free hour-long, one-on-one branding session as a prize for the most retweeted caption of the day. My own Twitter show runs seven days a week 365 days a year, although I limit the number of tweets I send over the weekends or holiday periods for obvious reasons.

Scheduling Your Tweets

If you want a 24-hour Twitter presence for your brand, it's essential to automatically schedule at least some of your tweets each day. Many of the popular Twitter clients such as TweetDeck and HootSuite have built-in scheduling tools, as shown in Figure 8-6, or you can use an external service such as Buffer (see Figure 8-7) that I describe later in this chapter.

Try to schedule an even balance of tweets throughout the day, but don't just post and forget about them! As I've mentioned, joining in the conversations you create and sharing them with others is a huge part of getting the most out of Twitter for your brand. Content may be king on Twitter, but engagement is undoubtedly his queen.

The schedule in Table 8-1 has blocked my daily show's tweets into three four-hour segments. If you wanted your daily show to start at 7 a.m. each day, the first tweet in this block would be scheduled for 7 a.m., with the other tweets going out in semiregular intervals of 25 to 90 minutes, depending on the number of tweets you intend to send. Obviously, the more tweets you feature in your show, the less time you need to leave between them when scheduling.

It's a good idea when starting out to experiment with the number of tweets you use in your show each day to find what works best for you and

TABLE 8-1

Example of my daily Twitter personal brand show

Schedule	Tweet	Included Link or Attachment	Type
Part 1	Social Media Is a Contact Sport by @grattongirl	(personal blog post link)	Inform/Foundation Brand Anchor
	One Minute World News (video) @BBCWorld	http://www.bbc.co.uk/news/video_and_audio/	Share+Inform/ Foundation
	A revealing glimpse of Twitterphobia:	http://yfrog.com/18kdwihj	Foundation
	Increasing Brand Awareness with #NFC technology and Social Media by @grattonboy #teamgratton	http://ow.ly/6BYM4	Foundation Brand Anchor
Part 2	"Don't judge each day by the harvest you reap but by the seeds that you plant. ~Robert Louis Stevenson" #quote	N/A	Inform/Foundation
	Change is Good – But Don't Forget to Ask Why. Great article from @tScottCase	http://t.co/B8TJr320	Share+Inform Suggested
	How to Take Your Brand From Zero to 100,000 by @grattongirl via @TheTop10Blog #branding	http://vsb.li/xHZpss	Inform+Foundation Brand Anchor
	Action Fraud - Protect Yourself Against Online Fraud (video) Watch and RT #devilsdetails	http://ow.ly/ahVBm	Inform+Engage Suggested
Part 3	The future is always beginning now. ~Mark Strand #quote	N/A	Inform/Foundation
	How to Manage Your Money on the Web	(personal blog post link)	Inform/Foundation Brand Anchor
	Spread your message by "word of mouse" as well as word of mouth – Gratton and Gratton #teamgratton	http://goo.gl/XFzVk	Inform/Foundation Brand Anchor
	The @grattongirl Review is out! Top stories today via @ASuss49, @Hammerkit, P3Linz, @MichaelCrossann and @simorganphoto	http://t.co/evi6zqJL	Inform+Share Brand Anchor

FIGURE 8-6

Many popular Twitter clients like HootSuite have a built-in scheduling tool.

your audience in terms of planning, time management, and reciprocation. Also, bear in mind that you don't want to schedule anything that is likely to need a high-level of immediate engagement when you're not going to be on Twitter to participate in the conversation (overnight, for example), so let common sense prevail when making your scheduled content choices.

Making Twitter the Hub of Your Show

My example daily schedule shows how you can use Twitter as the central hub of your brand show to take your followers on a journey across *all* your social media platforms. It's a use of social media that Dean and I coined in 2010 as *cross-platform promotion* (CPP). It involves the synergetic

FIGURE 8-7

Buffer finds and schedules the best times for your tweets to go out in your target time zone.

use of our various social media platforms to reinforce our brand message, albeit with a mixture of information, humor, and shared personal moments. It's a cocktail of content that can be tailored to fit any personal brand statement, as I've shown in Chapter 7, and it's one that will not only keep your existing followers coming back for more but will steadily bring a wealth of new quality followers to your fold.

The Wisdom of Repeat Tweets

Repeating tweets is a contentious subject, but more and more users have adopted Twitter as a promotional tool and are seeing the virtues and the sense behind repeat tweets.

It was Guy Kawasaki who first introduced me to the benefits of repeating my tweets over a 24-hour period. He likened his Twitter stream to the news stations that cycle their stories many times throughout the day. The stations repeat their segments to ensure that as many people as possible have the chance to catch their features, and the same can be said for the tweets you send out. After all, few people monitor Twitter all day, so by tweeting something only once, a significant number of your followers are highly unlikely to see it.

But let common sense prevail when it comes to repeating your tweets — and don't overdo it!

Twitter frowns on duplicate tweets being sent from the same account within a four-hour period and so it may suspend these accounts due to the high probability of the tweets being spam. I generally repeat my tweets every six to eight hours due to the geographical variances between my followers and the differences in time zones (something that I explain further in Chapter 9). Repeating my tweets several times a day means that I can reach the maximum number of my followers, no matter where in the world they might be located. Using a tool such as the Buffer app to schedule your tweets based on those time zones you want to tweet within can attract the maximum amount of audience attention (see Figure 8-7).

The equation is simple: Repeat your tweets to extend the number of people who will see them (your *Twitter reach*) and ultimately the number who will click through to any content such as an article or image URL. Increasing your reach increases the chance of your tweets being shared and retweeted (your *Twitter amplification*).

Above all, putting your personal brand Twitter content together should be a fun and enjoyable experience that you get to repeat on a daily basis, so put on your producer's hat and make your experience an unmissable one.

"How can it be said I am alone
when all the world is here to look on me?"

—*A Midsummer Night's Dream*

A Geography Lesson: The Global Power of Twitter

Twitter is no doubt a force to be reckoned with given its power to grab the world's attention. It has been embraced globally as a channel for tweeting against injustice, especially by people in countries where freedom of speech would have previously been impossible. That's why there was a global uproar when Twitter announced its plan to censor certain tweets in certain counties, those that contain content deemed to be illegal by their governments. The move immediately prompted an international outcry, along with calls for a boycott from some users.

"Thank you for the #censorship, #twitter, with love from the governments of #Syria, #Bahrain, #Iran, #Turkey, #China, #Saudi, and friends," wrote Bjorn Nilsson, a Twitter user in Sweden.

Today, if someone posts a message that insults a country's monarchy or government, which is punishable by a jail term, it is blocked and unavailable to Twitter users in that country, although still visible elsewhere. What's more, Twitter users throughout the country in question are notified that something was removed: Where the tweet once would have been visible, it is now replaced with a gray box containing a clear note, as shown in Figure 9-1: "Tweet withheld. This tweet from @*username* has been withheld in: *whatever country it is*."

This is in stark contrast to the way Twitter was used during the Egyptian revolution of 2011. Twitter provided a platform for the frustrated civilians of Egypt to communicate and organize their revolt to overthrow the 29-year rule of President Muhammad Mubarak (see Figure 9-2). Mubarak's administration was aware of the impact social media was having and took measures to have both Twitter and Facebook completely blocked by January 26, 2011.

By then, there was little the government could do to stop the events that were set in motion. It could not silence the voices of those who demanded change and who had embraced a new form of media to echo their cries.

Tweet withheld

This Tweet from @Username has been withheld in: Country. Learn more

FIGURE 9-1

Twitter users in censored countries are notified that their tweets have been withheld if they are deemed illegal.

FIGURE 9-2

Twitter provided a powerful global platform for the Egyptian revolution of 2011.

But the later announcement of geographical censorship by Twitter signaled the choice that it clearly had to make about its own existence: Should it be a tool for free speech that can be used in defiance of governments, as happened during the Arab Spring protests? Or are its intentions that of a commercial nature, a tool that must obey the laws of the lands where it seeks to attract customers and make money?

My belief is that Twitter wants to be all things to all people, a point driven home to me by the fact that the company identifies the locations of its users by looking at the Internet Protocol (IP) addresses of their computers or phones. However, it also lets users manually set their location to "worldwide," which circumvents the blocking system entirely.

For example, a user in Iran can simply change his or her location setting to "worldwide" and see everything tweeted.

Tweet Dreams Are Made in the USA

Despite the recent moves by Twitter to prevent rocking any political boats globally, the evidence increasingly shows that the worldwide adoption of the platform is slowly shrinking any geographical communication gaps. After all, the philosophies of the American dream, the land where Twitter and Facebook began — that of freedom of speech and all the things the Declaration of Independence stands for — have been woven into the social web and are seeping into the cultures that were previously denied their empowerment.

Social media has undoubtedly transformed the world into a multicultural global village; some would say one that has ironed out any cultural differences among us. Certainly on a conscious level we all seem to be tweeting from the same unified page, but there is another level that you need to understand to fully empower your personal brand with the knowledge needed to capture the widest global-audience possible.

Seeing the World through Culture-Colored Lenses

If you think about your Twitter followers in tribal terms, sectioning them into cultural groups, you may believe that the differences are slight. Our conscious behavior patterns support this, but culture isn't a conscious element alone. Sure, people align themselves with others from the same geographical tribes, seeking out followers from towns and places they can relate to; on Twitter, like everywhere else, we like to find and connect with our birds of a feather.

But when factors like language barriers (which I explain later in this chapter) and class system are removed, are there really any boundaries stopping us from connecting with everyone, everywhere?

On a conscious level, perhaps no! But let's shift our field of vision to consider the values, traditions, beliefs, and shared experiences that people carry with them unconsciously. By looking at social media behavior through these lenses, you'll see profound cultural differences that influence both behavior and opinion.

East Meets West — Or Does It?

Factors such as cultural interdependency vary dramatically from culture to culture. For example, in many Eastern cultures, families play an important part in the day-to-day support structure of one another, sharing housing and intergenerational living. This is in stark contrast to Western society, where it is commonplace for families to scatter across cities, states, or even countries, and for different generations in a family to live independently of one another's support.

This is not only a state of living, it is a state of mind. One that has been defined by Markus and Kitayama in their 1991 study on cultural variance, as "independent and interdependent self-construal." In it, they conclude that the influence of nurtured culture dramatically affects behavior and communication patterns. So are we all unconsciously relating to our Twitter posts in a different way, depending on our internal cultural constructs?

A 2011 white paper, "Global Social Media Challenge," by the research group Lewis Pulse suggests that cultural differences are still very much alive and kicking in social media and claims that "people from different nationalities react to social media in a way that has been predicted by social science."

It found that countries such as the U.K, and the Netherlands, both Western cultures, showed a particular lack of willingness to accept authority. It also revealed that the Dutch in particular were extremely skeptical of corporate content and weren't afraid to voice their opinions through their social networks. In complete contrast, the study found that those from Eastern cultures were generally more restrained overall in voicing any opinions that might rock the political or corporate boat.

To a psychologist, this is all fascinating, but how can these findings be used to empower your personal brand on a global scale?

Taking Your Brand Global

Despite any unconscious cultural biases, there has undoubtedly been a coming together of the independent and interdependent self-construals through the Twittersphere. Building emotional links to our fellow tweeters cross-culturally is like finding the ying to our yang in terms of depth of follower diversity and, ultimately, depth of engagement.

You probably wouldn't be on Twitter if local community connections were all that interested you. You're reading this book because you know that today, successful brands (of all sizes) need to spread their message through *word of mouse* as well as word of mouth. So here are some exercises you can do to help get you started building a global presence for brand "you."

1. Observe and report

Social media has been around only a few years, but it continues to evolve. I've observed how Twitter in particular has grown in different countries at different rates. I've noticed the different directions users take on certain social media platforms, and I carefully follow the issues where cultural differences inevitably clash.

Monitoring how businesses and brands in other countries use social media can be an enlightening process, one that can inspire you to try out new ideas to spread your personal brand message. Monitoring also lets you spot new trends in other areas of the world, which might in time affect your own industry.

Be creative in how you source this information and be prepared to dedicate time for research. There are a variety of tools you can use, including Twitter's search tools, websites, blogs, forums, videos, and podcasts.

Look for differences in web maturity, local infrastructure, and online habits, as these affect how users from other countries interact with social media on a daily basis and provide a useful indicator of what content they are looking for.

2. Don't assume anything

We make assumptions based on our own personal reality, which is perfectly understandable. The trouble is that everyone has a different window on his or her view of reality, and what may seem perfectly natural to one person may seem completely alien to another.

A brand can't survive in international business if it doesn't embrace diversity. Cultural differences will continue to arise that provide challenges to our brand messages. The way to move forward is by not letting these cultural differences create barriers. You can thrive in an international environment only when you accept and embrace other people's differences.

Embracing cultural awareness means accepting that you don't know everything. It means acknowledging that you may have already acquired some false assumptions about other cultures as a result of naïveté or propaganda that have no basis in fact. Prejudice and prejudgments, whether conscious or unconscious, are a huge barrier to getting to know and understand different cultures, so embark upon your research with an open mind.

3. Give yourself a brand checkup

Without a doubt, the most successful international professionals I know are the ones with the clearest understanding of their own values, cultural baggage, and general self-awareness. In fact, throughout my years in international marketing, I was always aware that my strong sense of self-knowledge and belief in my own brand was a key factor in my brand-building success stories for others.

You see, when you know exactly where your personal limits are, the personal boundaries you have, and the value you put on your personal baggage, it is very easy to communicate strategically with others. Your self-knowledge has removed any psychological barriers that could get in the way of you achieving your goals.

So give yourself a reality check from time to time and make sure that you're as resolute about your personal brand message today as you were on Day One. Regularly revisit it and revise it if necessary to incorporate any new values or considerations you may have picked up on your global journey of discovery. Think of it as your regular brand checkup.

A Question of Language

When looking at the aspect of language, the first question you need to ask yourself is whether your personal brand needs translation.

With English being the dominant language in the social sphere, it's actually quite easy to overlook the language aspect of your brand-messaging strategy. Having said that, your Twitter followers may not always tweet in English. In fact, you might want to follow non-English-speaking tweeters if they're connected to or influential in your field in some way that makes them valuable to your personal brand.

There are interesting aspects to language use in social media that are worth paying attention to when engaging with a global audience. One of these is the concept of the *borderless social web*, where followers can converse freely with others in their native tongues, regardless of whether it is English, French, or Chinese, thereby removing any language borders, as the term "borderless" suggests.

The Twitter Translation Center

Twitter has recognized and embraced this need and has developed the Twitter Translation Center to make borderless engagement a reality. It is continually calling on volunteer translators to take those tweets and

FIGURE 9-3

The Twitter Translation Center promotes borderless engagement through conversation among global Twitter users in their native languages.

links on Twitter that interest them and translate them for speakers of their native languages to enjoy across the globe (see Figure 9-3).

Once volunteers sign in to the Twitter Translation Center, they can start contributing to projects, including Twitter.com, Twitter's mobile apps, Twitter Help, and Twitter for Business. The center also includes a leader board of top translators, along with a level system to encourage both community and competition between translators.

Google Translate

Although not linked to Twitter, Google Translate (see Figure 9-4) is an amazing tool that uses advanced translation technology. By looking for patterns in documents that have already been translated by human translators, Google Translate makes intelligent guesses for approximate translations.

Although not all translations are perfect, this tool is constantly evolving and growing as it learns more from human-translated documents. To use it, simply copy and paste your tweet into Google Translate at translate.google.com, define your required languages, and *voilà*!

You can then translate your reply or comment and copy and paste it back into Twitter to continue the conversation in that language.

Twinslator

Twinslator (see Figure 9-5) is a free Twitter app that twins your tweet from your original language to your desired language and then gives you the option to tweet them both simultaneously.

FIGURE 9-4

Google Translate is a quick, easy, and sufficiently accurate translation tool.

FIGURE 9-5

Twinslator provides a clutter-free direct-to-Twitter translation experience.

From its minimalistic home page (www.twinslator.com), you simply type in your tweet and then select one of 42 languages from the pop-up menu before clicking the Translate button. You can opt to send only the translated tweet or both the original and the translated tweets.

Twanslate

Twanslate is an experimental add-on for the Mozilla Firefox browser that translates an incoming tweet from a variety of different languages into English. Using Google's Translate service, the Firefox add-on functions as a simple icon button (a little globe icon) below any tweet in another language. You simply click on the icon button to translate that particular tweet into English, as shown in Figure 9-6.

Twitter Auto-Translate

Twitter is beta-testing an auto-translation tool based on Microsoft's Bing Translator, which supports 38 languages. With the translator, you can click on a non-English tweet and view the translated version immediately below it.

Twitter began rolling out this feature to a small percentage of accounts in February 2012; broad availability is expected by 2013.

FIGURE 9-6

Twanslate is a Firefox add-on that translates your tweets using Google Translate directly in Twitter.

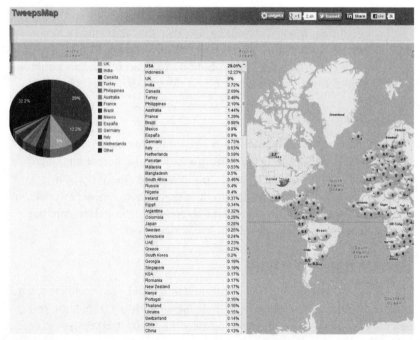

FIGURE 9-7

TweetsMap lets you see your followers from a geographical perspective.

Tweeting for Time Zones

I explain the benefits of repeat tweets in Chapter 8 as part of your personal brand show on Twitter, and there's no better rationale for this than the time zone differences you need to consider when planning a cross-cultural strategy.

Get to understand your most active global communities by breaking them down into clearly defined sections, country by country. Then map them visually, using tools such as TweepsMap (see Figure 9-7) or Map My Followers, both free follower-mapping apps. (Note that Map My Followers works only for Twitter accounts with fewer than 50,000 followers.)

You can then use tools such as Buffer, which I cover in Chapter 8, to find the best possible times to schedule your tweets for each group, based on location.

"None will sweat but for promotion."

—*As You Like It*

10

Beyond Hashtags: Make Your Brand a Trending Topic

Girls may prefer diamonds, but hashtags are undoubtedly a tweet's best friend. They are the little promoters that grab your followers' attention and lead them back to your latest and greatest post.

"Need a great #inspirational #quote? Here's one for you!" they exclaim. "Looking for information on #Superbowl #tickets? Then follow me!"

A carefully thought-out hashtag can significantly amplify the social audience reach of any tweet you send.

But how do you effectively use hashtags on Twitter to link and draw people to your conversations?

Well, let's start with the basics. When you place the # symbol before a word, phrase, or abbreviation on Twitter, it creates a mini conversation that can be looked up and followed. Hashtags organize tweets by conversation and raise the online visibility of brands, events, promotions, and more. The more exposure your tweets have on Twitter, the more opportunities you have of building a large and quality following for your personal brand.

But is there any scientific research to support their effectiveness in raising a brand profile?

Well, yes! In 2011, marketing solutions company LevelWing looked at almost 450 tweeted messages for three Twitter handles over one month, comparing the clickthrough rates of tweets with hashtags to a website, article, or other brand-related link against those without hashtags.

Hashtags used throughout the month varied, but always included the words that the target audience associated with the products or services offered by the brands behind the Twitter accounts. What they found was consistent across all three accounts: Overall, when compared to non-hashtagged messages, hashtags resulted in higher engagement in terms of clickthroughs to the brand links.

- Account 1: 5 percent increased clickthrough rate

> Account 2: 11 percent increased clickthrough rate
> Account 3: 11 percent increased clickthrough rate

That's an average of 9 percent increased clickthrough success rate using hashtags — a significant amount, especially when you consider how many people there might be in your social audience.

Remember that people don't even have to follow you on Twitter to see your hashtag there; they simply have to search for something that interests them. So, if you start thinking of hashtags as the equivalent of keywords on Google, you can begin to see just how incredibly powerful they can be.

Your Fail-Safe Guide to Using Hashtags

Here's my step-by-step guide to lifting and promoting your personal brand through the incorporation of effective hashtags on Twitter.

1. Learn how Twitter hashtags work

Check your tweets and notice where your most influential follows are using hashtags. The best way to understand the philosophy behind the placement of a hashtag is to click on it and follow its conversation on Twitter.

Simply click any hashtag that interests you to get to the Twitter search page, where you'll see a stream of conversations relating to the hashtag word. You can find out what the hashtag is being used for, who is using it, and links to where you can get more information. It's a great way to get started, and gives you an outside-in perspective of how hashtags are most effectively being used.

2. Use unique hashtags for your own brand tweets

Having done a little research, it's time to take action and start using hashtags for your own brand on Twitter. But, before including a unique hashtag, look it up to ensure that it's not being used in other tweets. And if it's not being used, think about whether the word will have meaning to your followers without an explanation. For example, an event such as the Super Bowl will have a hashtag that speaks for itself, whereas your brand hashtag may not be so obvious in meaning.

FIGURE 10-1

I use several related hashtags to promote this book on Twitter.

So, if your hashtag isn't clear, make sure it hits home by providing an explanation to your followers, as I've done with mine for the #FollowMe promotion tweets for this book (see Figure 10-1).

In my #FollowMe promotion, I also incorporated several popular hashtags in my tweets, such as #book and #Twitter. This way, I can be sure that people looking for a new book on Twitter were likely to come across my tweet for *Follow Me*.

While researching the hashtag term you're considering, look at how it's being used across Twitter, as well as how often it's being used. What might sound like a great keyword to you may be used more frequently in a completely different context — even a negative context, which is not something you want associated with your brand.

3. Organize your event hashtags

Conferences and events rely on the hashtag system more than almost any other Twitter tool. It's now become standard to track conversations regarding speakers and after parties via a hashtag. The key factors to remember when using them in this way are:

Choose your hashtag early

This may seem an easy task, but it's one that is imperative to get right. As I've mentioned, be sure to choose a simple hashtag that represents your event or brand as effectively as possible; but, bear in mind Twitter's 140-character limit. For example, if your event is the The Business Tweet Awards 2013, you wouldn't want to use #businesstweetawards2013 as your hashtag. Although relevant, it uses far too many characters, so instead think about shortening it in a way that still makes sense — something like #biztweets2013.

Make sure your attendees know it

Once your event hashtag is out there, use it whenever you tweet about the event, as well as including it on your website, referring to it in the opening remarks, and mentioning throughout the day of the event itself. Keep reminding attendees to use your hashtag so you can all track the conversation through it and keep the momentum going.

Provide a hashtag tool for nontweeters

It's hard to believe, I know, but there may be some event attendees that aren't on Twitter yet! To keep them included in the conversation, you can use a widget to insert the Twitter stream containing your hashtag on your website. Who knows, it may even encourage them to jump on Twitter as a new follower!

You can incorporate this stream quickly and simply on your website using tools such as the free Twitter widget, shown in Figure 10-2.

FIGURE 10-2

Twitter provides a widget that works with any website and is a great way to enable nontweeters to see the conversation around your event.

4. Learn from the media

Whether it's a popular TV show or a Sunday night football game, the media have become expert at incorporating brand hashtags in their screenings, to allow the audience to give feedback and join in the conversation about their shows on Twitter.

For example, *American Horror Story* displays the hashtag #AHS during commercials for viewers to add to their tweets about the show. This exercise has dramatically increased tweets going out about prime-time shows, and no doubt has increased viewing rates as a result.

Another trick used by the media with great success is using hashtags at key moments during the program itself, as NBC did to great effect with *The Voice* (see Figure 10-3).

5. Generate a call to action

You can also use hashtags to generate a call to action for a particular brand promotion or for a forthcoming competition or event you are hosting. A great example is the question posed by CNN during its

FIGURE 10-3

NBC used the hashtag #TheVoice at key moments during the TV show to great effect in terms of viewer response.

coverage of the recent British royal wedding. It asked viewers to tweet their theory behind America's fascination with the royal nuptials, using both the hashtags #CNNTV (the media brand) and #RoyalWedding (the event) to create a buzz and generate a sense of community in CNN's Twitter audience. Figure 10-4 shows how this call to action was televised.

You can use the same principles as CNN in any brand videos and images you post links to on Twitter or feature on your website or other promotional material — even your business cards! Be creative, and remember that the aim is to generate a two-way conversation with everything you do using hashtags.

Making It Trend

We all want our hashtag to become the next trending topic, the one that everyone's talking about. But, as smaller brands, how do you achieve this? Can your latest hashtag find its way into thousands, even millions

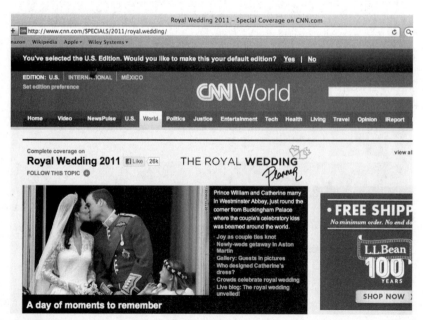

FIGURE 10-4

Generate a call to action by involving your audience using hashtags, as CNN did during the royal wedding in 2011.

of tweets? The answer is yes, it *is* possible. But to achieve this level of success, you need to know the factors behind what makes a trending topic on Twitter.

1. Make volume your focus

Put quite simply, the key to making your hashtag trend is to maximize the number of people who incorporate it in their tweets. And of course, the whole equation is relative to the number of people active on Twitter.

So, with this in mind, it's better to have 100 people tweet about a single hashtag less frequently than have five people tweet the same hashtag more frequently.

In terms of what trends, it's the volume — or number — of people tweeting that is the primary focus.

2. Work with your time zones

In Chapter 8, I explore the importance of reaching as many people as possible through clever scheduling of your tweets, and the need to incorporate as many time zones as possible at optimum times. So work with your audience to ensure that you reach the people who will be most interested in retweeting your hashtag.

As I've just explained, volume is what really counts when creating trends. So see what the trending topics are at the moment and study when and where they go out throughout the day around the world. Look for as many connections with the current trending topics to link to your hashtag, without losing its relevancy. These links will act like a magnet for your hashtag and will encourage its inclusion in trending topics' tweets.

3. Use your influencers

Use the key influencers in your following to become convincers for your hashtag by getting them interested and involved in what you are trying to achieve. Clearly, there has to be a carrot for them in the form of benefits for their own brand, so find ways to connect what they do with what you are trying to achieve and ask for their help in spreading the word.

Bear in mind, though, that a favor acted on is a favor owed, so be sure to return their support when you can and, whatever you do, don't exploit their friendship by continually badgering them for help.

FIGURE 10-5

Take a leaf out of Samsung's book and give your followers the chance to win a prize based on the use of your hashtag (left). It took #samsungcheerdance to the Number One trending topic spot overnight (right).

4. Offer a reward

This is a great strategy, one that can make your hashtags quickly trend if you can pull it off effectively. People love rewards, so the chance to win something through the use of your hashtag is a great incentive that can see it spread like wildfire.

Think about what you can offer. For example, you could run a quiz, where you ask questions relating to your brand sector and then reward the top answers tweeted with your hashtag. If you can afford it, sweeten the promotion further by offering a prize that is a pulling factor for others. Take a lesson from Samsung's book, which made its hashtag #samsungcheerdance a trending topic overnight by offering its latest phone as a prize for a cheer-leading competition it was sponsoring (see Figure 10-5).

You may of course come up with something better than a quiz. Just start thinking about ways to get more people interested, think outside of the box for what people are looking for in your audience sectors, and, above all, give people something to participate in and enjoy.

By following these methods and thinking creatively about how your personal brand message can translate into great hashtags, you are well on your way to becoming the next trending topic.

Part Three

Twitter Branding Showcase Stories

IN THIS PART

Twitter superstars understand their personal brands from the inside out, embrace their power, and know how to make themselves shine in the Twitterverse.

Twitter Branding Superstars

All the social media superstars in this part have mastered the art of personal branding using Twitter in a way that truly wows!

The chapters that follow feature individual success stories, revealing their initial thoughts about Twitter and explaining the lessons they learned along their path to social media success.

The chapters are broken into sections that walk you through every aspect of their journey, from their introduction to the platform to how they chose to build their personal brand with it. The chapters also provide these superstars' golden rules to success, along with the Twitter tools they use on a daily basis.

This part provides you with unique and never-before-revealed secrets to personal branding success on Twitter. I hope that you find reading it as inspiring as I have in compiling it.

"Sparing people the need for surgery one at a time :-(
Need an app for this!!!"

@hjluks

11

Empowering Health Care

Howard J. Luks, M.D., is far more than just a great physician. Named as one of "Twitter's Top Ten Doctors," as well as one of the "Eleven Faces to Follow in Health Care and Social Media" by FierceHealthIT, Howard is testimony to the changing face of health care using social media as a platform to educate and empower his patients.

He's approachable and likable, and he enjoys lively banter with his followers but beyond that, his personal brand is one of education, reassurance, and empowerment — three things that today's health care system desperately needs to impart to the wider community.

Howard has managed, through clever and insightful use of his social networks, to blur the somewhat starchy boundaries that have traditionally existed between doctor and patient. His daily tweets (@hjluks) provide the perfect *edutainment* blend of fact, humor, and reciprocation.

What's more, Howard knows how to involve his audience on a personal level, using everything from asking for advice on his medical conference speeches to sharing favorite family and leisure time moments (see Figure 11-1).

It's interesting to note that social media use among physicians is actually higher than among consumers in general, as discovered by a CSC study in 2011. Surprisingly, though, the study went on to report that most physicians are using social media in their personal but not professional lives.

Howard sees this trend as something that needs to change, not only to empower patients but also physicians themselves. He believes, as research supports, that by embracing social media, doctors could reduce their workloads by moving some of the interactions now on the phone or in the office to social media platforms.

He says, "Important changes are taking place that will forever change the way the physicians and patients interact. Shared-decision-making principles, the

FIGURE 11-1

Howard J. Luks, M.D., involves his Twitter audience on a personal as well as professional level.

concept of informed choice versus informed consent and the desires of the participatory medicine movement, will dramatically alter the health care landscape."

Wen-ying Sylvia Chou, the program director for the National Cancer Institute's Health Communication and Informatics Research Branch, shares this view, claiming, "The democratization of information through social media is shaping clinical encounters and the patient-provider relationship." It's a statement that firmly resonates through the spectrum of social media platforms used by Howard on a daily basis.

Twitter as a Springboard

Twitter plays a key role in Howard's use of social media. He sees it as very much a springboard to his other platforms such as YouTube, where he hosts a channel providing a wealth of informative videos explaining treatment options and procedures for a variety of orthopedic conditions (see Figure 11-2). It's this effective use of cross-platform promotion (CPP) that sets Howard apart from many other physicians using social media.

So how did Howard get started on Twitter, and how did he use it to build such a successful personal brand?

Starting Out

Howard was an early adopter of Twitter, signing up for his account back in 2008. As not only a tech-savvy physician but also a social person

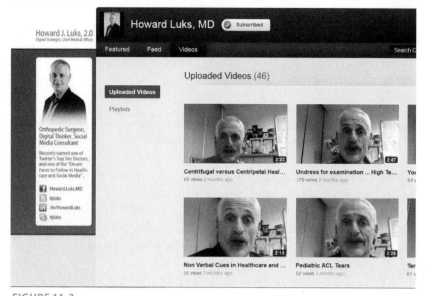

FIGURE 11-2

Many of Howard's tweets link to his YouTube videos, which cover a variety of patient conditions and concerns.

in general, he was both intrigued by the platform's potential and keen to try new ways to connect with others.

"I was communicating with, learning from, and teaching people I never would have otherwise met from across the globe. As I started to enjoy using Twitter for my own knowledge, curation, or simple after-hours banter, I started to delve into how Twitter could be useful as a means of fostering my relevance and extending my reach beyond the four walls of my practice."

This need to extend his reach, inspired Howard to begin sharing content on Twitter using cross-platform promotion to incorporate links to his blog, website, YouTube, and other channels (see Figure 11-3).

As the platform began to mature, other physicians, patients, and health care professionals started to appear on Twitter, so Howard began to organize live chats around various topics in health care, as shown in Figure 11-4.

Howard recalls first starting these revolutionary collaborations on Twitter: "We studied and discussed the impact of the mobile health

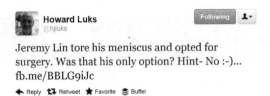

Howard Luks
@hjluks

Jeremy Lin tore his meniscus and opted for surgery. Was that his only option? Hint- No :-)...
fb.me/BBLG9iJc

← Reply ⇄ Retweet ★ Favorite ≋ Buffer

FIGURE 11-3

A great example of Howard's use of CPP on Twitter, where he links to another of his social media platforms to provide additional information

initiatives, behavioral modification, improving compliance with post-visit or discharge instructions, and other similar issues."

As a result of his endeavors, key innovators and entrepreneurs in the health care sector began to take notice, and gradually Howard's online interactions evolved into long-term authentic relationships.

Howard Luks' Golden Rules for Personal Branding Success

Howard describes his personal brand on Twitter as one that is continually evolving: "My goal is to not only educate patients and my fellow colleagues but to assist entrepreneurs seeking to springboard off Twitter to other useful activities to help physicians in their daily practice."

Howard's incredible personal branding success stems from his desire to "support the spread of meaningful, trustworthy, evidence based (when available), actionable information, and guidance to patients and consumers from around the world." He believes that physicians have a

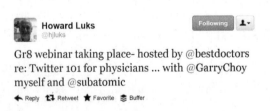

Howard Luks
@hjluks

Gr8 webinar taking place- hosted by @bestdoctors re: Twitter 101 for physicians ... with @GarryChoy myself and @subatomic

← Reply ⇄ Retweet ★ Favorite ≋ Buffer

FIGURE 11-4

An example of the revolutionary way Howard began using Twitter for live chats and expert collaboration

FIGURE 11-5

Howard has dramatically extended his outreach by providing links on Twitter to treatment guidebooks for patients.

moral obligation to provide quality content and "to drown out the commercialized nonsense that exists online today."

Howard has used Twitter to humanize his practice and extend his outreach far beyond the four walls of his office (see Figure 11-5). This is ultimately his golden rule to personal branding success using Twitter. Others in his field are slowly emulating Howard's approach, which is no surprise, as he provides an excellent example of how to balance the flow of content and keep your Twitter stream interesting for followers.

Throughout his years on Twitter, Howard has tried many different approaches in content sharing, frequently incorporating personal tidbits to aid in humanizing both his personal brand and his practice, while enabling patients to become comfortable with him and what he has to offer or say before they enter his office.

Howard also shares content on Twitter to assist others in their interactions with their physicians even if they aren't his patients (see Figure 11-6) — he calls such people "part of a global patient population

Howard Luks
@hjluks   [Following] [👤▾]

How long is my recovery? That is a VERY
subjective topic! It will vary dramatically if you are
a couch potato... fb.me/YuioMSjD

↩ Reply   ⇄ Retweet   ★ Favorite   ⥯ Buffer

FIGURE 11-6

Howard is happy to offer advice even to followers who aren't his patients.

that has grown tired of the commercialized nonsense that exists in the online world and is instead looking for useful, meaningful and actionable information."

Ultimately, Howard firmly believes that all physicians on Twitter need to define their own personal goals and personal brand messages. "They need to experiment with what sticks and what simply passes through the stream untouched. Staying focused and staying engaged is the key to a successful Twitter outreach presence."

Howard believes that, at its heart, Twitter is about people, about relationships, and about communication. For him, it is about fostering his relevance and value as a physician and educator beyond the four walls of his practice. He believes that "establishing a digital footprint, rooted as a social media presence is about educating, engaging, growing your audience, improving outcomes, improving compliance, and potentially improving the bottom line of your practice."

Howard underlines his personal branding on Twitter with the philosophy that understanding your audience and staying true to the message you are trying to portray is essential. This knowledge then needs to translate itself into effective engagement, which Howard believes above all else is the key to Twitter success. "The worst mistake you can make is to put information or content on Twitter and fail to engage when someone responds."

Into the Future

Howard's personal brand was not built overnight, and he views success as something that happens on a long-term basis. He believes that many of the physician dropout rates occur on Twitter because of a lack of immediate return on investment (ROI).

"The most important lesson I have learned over the years is that you need to be honest with yourself and need to prepare before jumping into the social media waters. Building your brand through social media will not happen overnight — you will go through times where you want a short break and time off the grid, but you will pay the price for doing so."

Howard has found scheduling tools such as Buffer and HootSuite very useful. "They enable me to anticipate times when I may be busy and not able to tend to my various platforms as often as possible. I can then schedule my tweets to provide my personal brand with a permanent online presence."

Howard acknowledges that social capital and influence can be fleeting. He believes the most important lesson he has learned is to be honest, open, and transparent, letting people know the person behind the Twitter handle: "Let them decide whether or not the information you have to share is useful. Do not force yourself or overly promote yourself or your relative expertise. Instead let the people decide if you are worth following. If your content and your interactions are useful, they will follow you and they will share with their networks."

Howard is proud of the many memorable experiences that have been enabled by his personal-brand social media presence. He has appeared on national television and has been asked to share his experiences through high-profile speaking engagements. But he is equally proud of the small wins, too: "When you help a person understand that there is a global presence of engaged health care practitioners who are more than willing to help, it is wonderful to witness that lightbulb moment and know that you made a difference in that person's life or comforted them in their time of need."

Howard believes that Twitter will continue to evolve as the platform matures and the API is used by the community to build platforms and tools that provide active users an easier and more targeted means of engaging with and helping patients looking for information on their disease process or a quality physician to work with them.

Howard believes his own presence on Twitter will continue to mature as he discovers new ways of interacting with different patient communities, like-minded physicians, and organizations looking for guidance or assistance in navigating the social space (see Figure 11-7).

Howard also hopes that Twitter itself will evolve in a way that provides consumers and the physician community alike with a more

Howard Luks
@hjluks

Following

How Physicians Can Create A Personal Brand With Twitter | FEED The Agency j.mp/JRFhIe w/ @grattongirl (thk you!)

← Reply ⇄ Retweet ★ Favorite ⇌ Buffer

2
RETWEETS

1
FAVORITE

FIGURE 11-7

Howard has been instrumental in showing other physicians how to create a personal brand using Twitter; he was recently featured in my interview with the global health care marketing agency FEED.

useful and strategic means of using the platform for education outreach, learning, and sharing.

Howard successfully puts into practice all the steps to personal branding on Twitter that I cover in Chapter 8 as well as incorporating the four types of tweet that I introduce in Chapter 5. His is a true Twitter success story, and one that we can all learn from and be inspired by.

"Rocking the A-Z of Twitter and tweets"

@BobWarren

12

Changing the Job Market One Tweet at a Time

The first thing you notice about Bob Warren's Twitter presence is how his personal brand message leaps out at you in everything he tweets. His tweets ooze personality, one that's vibrant, charismatic, and above all passionate about his latest venture, ResumeBear (see Figure 12-1), an online service for job-seekers that puts them well and truly in control of their career endeavors.

Getting Started

Bob joined Twitter in 2008, shortly after launching ResumeBear. He was thrilled and excited about the change he could make for others in their job-search empowerment and wanted to get the word out to as many people as possible. He recalls, "Things were going well, but we needed a better way to get the word out about how fantastic our product was for job-seekers. A friend of mind said, 'Hey Bob, you should really check out Twitter.' I was already a big-time social media user and so immediately I saw the power of the Twitter platform."

Bob envisioned connecting with thousands of people who would be able to experience the benefits of ResumeBear and then spread the word through their own followers. It was a lightbulb moment, one that he hasn't looked back from:

"A couple of aspects in particular really attracted me to Twitter," Bob recalls. "The first aspect was that it was free; I saw it as free advertising. The second aspect was the community nature of Twitter. I could meet and connect with people who would have never had the opportunity to meet. Following someone's tweets is a great way to get to know people, see into their world and what activities they are engaged in."

FIGURE 12-1

ResumeBear's philosophy has become an integral part of Bob Warren's personal brand success story on Twitter.

Keeping It Real

Twitter allowed Bob to create friendships with people in his field of interest. These relationships grew over time to become mutually beneficial for him and his company, and Bob believes the reason for this lies in his brand's authenticity. In essence, with Bob, what you see is what you get. He's real, and the man behind the brand shines in every tweet he sends.

"When you are looking to brand yourself on Twitter, it is important to be genuine and show all your followers that you are a real person. I am who I am. If you were to meet me face to face, you'd see it's the same guy with 100,000-plus followers on Twitter. It's important to remember this because if you try to fake it, people will eventually see through you. Give them a glimpse of what you like to do, where you go, and stuff like that, but always remember what you are trying to accomplish on Twitter. Tweet with purpose and keep it real."

If you are planning to build a large following, it is important to always remember to provide something of value (see Figure 12-2). Bob has a great product with ResumeBear, but he wanted to provide more than just one tool for job-seekers, so he created a blog as well, which he markets using cross-platform promotion (CPP) on Twitter. Every day, Bob

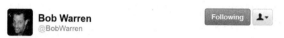

Bob Warren
@BobWarren
Following
Personal Branding – why a job seeker needs to do it bit.ly/o9iYzm
Reply Retweet Favorite Buffer

FIGURE 12-2

Bob's tweets resonate with his personal brand while adding value for his followers.

posts great articles that all job-seekers should read if they want to get ahead in the game.

"People love these articles, and Twitter is a great way to share them and remind people that we have something they need," he says.

With the help of Twitter, the ResumeBear blog has grown to be one of the most popular and important blogs for job-seekers and career development. Bob has embraced the fact that people bond best with things that fill a need or serve a purpose in their lives.

He realizes that you can't just tweet the address to a static website and expect people to click on it, but if you provide fresh content and ideas that people enjoy reading through CPP tweeting, your following on Twitter will increase and your blog traffic will rise (see Figure 12-3).

Bob's clever mix of content has made his personal brand Twitter show one that continues to grow in popularity.

"If you are providing good content, people will retweet your posts. We have a blog article that has been retweeted 140,000 times. That means 140,000 people liked an article enough to share it with all their friends and followers. That is the power of Twitter! This would have never happened if the content on our Twitter show weren't amazing. Make your tweets relevant to your followers. Provide information people want, and they will follow you."

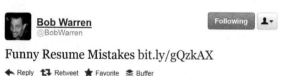

Bob Warren
@BobWarren
Following
Funny Resume Mistakes bit.ly/gQzkAX
Reply Retweet Favorite Buffer

FIGURE 12-3

Bob's clever mix of Twitter content keeps his followers entertained and educated.

FIGURE 12-4

Bob realizes that the short, thoughtful tweets can be the most powerful of all.

Sharing the Twitter Love

Bob also takes the time to show that he cares about his followers. He knows the power of reciprocation and engagement, and he understands that those short, thoughtful tweets can prove to be the most powerful of all, as shown in Figure 12-4.

Bob is on Twitter a lot! You can see by his total tweets (62,000 and counting) that he never goes long without tweeting or acknowledging those who retweet him or share news that he believes his followers will enjoy.

"I always find the time to spread the retweet love for friends. It's this sharing that keeps the heart of Twitter constantly beating," he says.

Bob's philosophy is to keep his personal brand message simple through his use of Twitter. He doesn't use many Twitter tools or applications; he likes to tweet and retweet manually and in real time wherever possible. But Bob does use widgets on his blog and website that make retweeting by others an easy task, as shown in Figure 12-5.

FIGURE 12-5

Bob uses a widget on his website and blog that allows readers to easily retweet and share his content.

Bob is also a great fan of hashtags, finding them "a fun way to say hello and that I'm thinking about you." He acknowledges the fact that "people love to hear from you, even if it's just a simple 'have a great day!'"

Above all, no matter how big Bob's personal brand has become through Twitter, he's never forgotten how to be social and appreciative to his followers. He reminds himself on a daily basis to keep a sense of balance and not to "get so caught up in sharing your own content and serving your own agenda that you forget about being social. It is a social media platform, after all. Say hi to people and let them know you are around and care about them."

Bob Warren's Golden Rules for Personal Branding Success

Bob's experience has led him to these insights on what works best for personal branding on Twitter:

1. Be yourself.
2. Keep your brand show entertaining through your Twittertorial calendar.
3. Always add value.
4. Follow the influencers in your field.
5. Retweet others.
6. Tweet with a purpose.
7. Keep it real.
8. Stay humble.
9. Use the four types of tweets every day.
10. Have fun!

"You are what you tweet!"

@adamsconsulting

13

Making Twitter Your Personal Brand Diary

"Twitter is like a diary for me," says Diana Adams. "I can look back through my timeline and know exactly what I was thinking and feeling on the days I sent certain tweets."

Certainly looking at Diana's Twitter stream (see Figure 13-1), you can immediately get a sense of the witty, superintelligent, and sometimes cheeky lady behind the tweets. Diana's personal brand Twitter show radiates all the things that she loves, that she admires, and that simply catch her attention at a particular moment.

Founder of the #BA75 (that's short for Badass 75 Women of Twitter, of which I'm proud to be one), Diana certainly knows how to strut her proverbial stuff on Twitter. As a researcher and writer for BitRebels.com, her curation skills are second to none, and she has a way of hitting exactly the right notes with her followers in providing both value and entertainment, a rare combination that Diana manages to achieve almost effortlessly, it seems.

So what's the story behind Diana's personal brand success?

First-Tweet Nerves

Diana remembers hearing about Twitter for the first time in December 2008, but she didn't sign up to use the service until March 9, 2009. She recalls, "I heard people talking about Twitter and how interesting it was to type 140-character messages to people in the form of what everyone now knows as a tweet. I had never used a social media site before Twitter. Social media as a whole was still in its infancy, and Facebook was the only really popular social media site at the time. I wasn't on Facebook, and I had no idea what to expect when I got on Twitter. I followed a handful of people and then sat back in amazement as I watched my Twitter stream for the first time.

Diana Adams
@adamsconsulting

How To: Be Awesome On Twitter - bit.ly/eF

← Reply ⟲ Retweet ★ Favorite ≋ Buffer

8:38 PM - 12 May 12 via Rebel Tweet · Embed this Tweet

FIGURE 13-1

Diana Adams carries through her charismatic and fun-loving personal brand message in everything she tweets.

"I just tried to watch and learn how other people tweeted before I actually sent a tweet myself. I saw people using the RT and quickly learned that is a retweet. Twitter is like anything else, if you really want to learn about it, which I did, it's not hard to pick up. You just have to put a little effort into it. The first time someone sent me a tweet and the first time I was retweeted were both huge events for me. I remember jumping up and down with a big smile on my face."

In the beginning, Diana says she didn't have any thoughts about how useful Twitter would be from a personal branding perspective. "I don't think very many people thought about it that way back then. ... It was still so new, and at that time, none of us really understood what a powerful platform it would quickly evolve into. After about six months, the reality of what Twitter was capable of started to sink in."

Back when Diana signed up, Twitter was a really small community, and it wasn't very hard to make an impact. People were hungry for information, just like they are now, and it didn't take long before she was completely hooked. Now, Diana has sent more than 112,000 tweets, and her popularity and influence on the platform continues to grow.

Fine-Tuning Her Personal Brand on Twitter

Diana learned how to use Twitter for her personal brand by trial and error. There were no user guides as such in the early days of Twitter and the platform was still very much in its infancy, so Diana was still feeling her way.

"I learned so much about personal branding when I set up my Twitter profile. The thing is, once you have established your personal brand with your username, it's tough to change it. Some people have done it very successfully, like @AnitaNelson, @GlenGilmore, and @lorimcneeartist. They are all high-profile Twitter users, and all three changed their usernames to be more personal, but it can be risky.

"When I set up my Twitter account, I set it up as @adamsconsulting because I am the co-owner of an Apple-certified consulting company in Atlanta called Adams Consulting Group. At the time, that seemed like a logical username. In retrospect, I wish so much that I had used my name instead. I would have loved to have the username @Diana_Adams."

But as time went on, Diana decided that to change her username would be a mistake. "I have so much time and hard work invested in @adamsconsulting, and that username has a whole reputation that's already built. My entire personal brand is wrapped up in the username and I now have the same username on Facebook, Google+, and Pinterest. At this point, I've decided not to change it."

Diana's philosophy of personal branding in social media is all about building relationships in what has become a new value economy. This means letting followers see as much of the "real you" as possible through your bio (see Figure 13-2).

"If you are using Twitter to build your personal brand," Diana says, "it's vital to complete all the information that Twitter asks in the bio section. It's important to have a profile picture, a complete bio, a link, and a location. Personal branding in social media is about building relationships, networking, meeting new friends, and helping one another. It's hard to do that successfully if you don't allow people to view you as a

Diana Adams

@adamsconsulting FOLLOWS YOU

Graduate of USC, Entrepreneur for 10 yrs, BitRebels.com,
Co-Founder of #BA75, I'm really into just being happy. Big fan of
Caramel Macchiatos & Star Wars. #geek

Atlanta, Georgia, USA · http://www.AdamsConsultingGroup.com

FIGURE 13-2

Diana's bio reveals the fun-loving, happy lady behind the personal brand.

Part Three: *Twitter Branding Showcase Stories*

FIGURE 13-3

Diana's Twitter profile picture at left shows the @adamsconsulting brand we know and love. But her dramatic change to her Twitter profile picture (right) proved to be detrimental to her personal brand.

real person. Every piece of your Twitter profile will help you build your brand, so use it all to your advantage."

Diana also learned a lesson about keeping consistency in your brand profile, especially where her profile picture was concerned. She recalls, "I had a very interesting experience regarding my personal branding on Twitter. I like to change my hair color a lot. It seems like a trivial thing, but in a profile picture, it can be a big deal. I had always heard people talk about how important it is to be genuine on Twitter, and that includes your profile picture.

"In my original Twitter photo, my hair is auburn [see Figure 13-3]. After I colored it blonde one day, I changed my picture so that it would be current [see Figure 13-3]," she recalls.

What happened next surprised her. "Suddenly people couldn't find my tweets in their Twitter stream because they were looking for my regular profile picture. I received tweets from people saying that the change was weird, and I even had someone tweet me and say that he felt strange tweeting with me because I was suddenly like a different person. I could go on and on, but the lesson here is that people get attached to avatars, and from a personal branding perspective, you don't want to lose the trust you've built with people just because you changed your picture. After only two days, I felt the backlash of my avatar change so much that I changed it back to the original one.

"I'm not saying that I won't change my photo again. After all, I don't want to be 50 years old someday and have the same profile picture I have now, but next time the change will be subtle. I will not do a drastic change to my photo ever again. I definitely learned my lesson on that one!"

Addicted to Twitter

"I'm a Twitter addict," Diana claims (see Figure 13-4), "so my experience with Twitter might be a lot different from most people. Aside from an eight-day period in 2010 when I had a serious case of social media burnout, I've been on Twitter every single day since I signed up for the service on March 9, 2009.

"A lot of people set aside 15 minutes in the morning or evening to tweet. I don't use Twitter that way. I've incorporated Twitter into my lifestyle, so I don't set aside time to tweet. Instead, I tweet whenever all day long. For example, if I'm on hold for someone on the phone, I'll send a tweet. If I'm standing in line at the store, I'll send a tweet. If I'm in the bathtub or even if I'm riding my bicycle and I think of something funny, I'll send a tweet [see Figure 13-5]. I sleep with my iPhone under my pillow, so during the night if I wake up, I'll send a tweet."

As far as content goes, Diana writes a minimum of three articles on BitRebels.com every day, seven days a week, which she tweets links to, again embracing cross-platform promotion (CPP).

"I'm humbled to say that our blog recently reached a Twitter milestone. We've been retweeted more than a million times. I also tweet other content that I find, plus retweeting is important to me. It's a way to give back on Twitter, and I retweet a lot."

Diana Adams
@adamsconsulting

Are We REALLY Addicted To Social Media? [Infographic] - bit.ly/eG5Z4b

← Reply ⟲ Retweet ★ Favorite ≋ Buffer

6:15 PM - 2 May 12 via Rebel Tweet · Embed this Tweet

FIGURE 13-4

Diana makes no secret of the fact that she's a Twitter addict and even jokes about it with her followers.

Diana Adams
@adamsconsulting

How To: Twitter & Ride Your Bike At The Same
Time - bit.ly/spuifw

← Reply   ↻ Retweet   ★ Favorite   ≋ Buffer

FIGURE 13-5

Diana has even been known to tweet while riding her bicycle.

Diana Adams' Golden Rules for Personal Branding Success

Diana has ten best practices for successful personal branding.

1. Know your brand

"Before you start promoting your brand on Twitter, be sure you know what your personal brand is. If you don't feel confident about your brand message, and if you can't describe your brand in one or two sentences, you might want to think about refining it a little.

"My personal brand is wrapped around everything that is considered geek, and I attract the geeky crowd on Twitter. I'm known for tweeting about Star Wars, Lego, geeky apps, and social media.

"What is your brand? Do people see your profile picture and immediately think of your brand? If not, that's your goal. If even you are unclear about your brand, the first thing you want to do is develop your brand identity. What is your passion? What do you want to tweet about? What is your blog about? In what areas could you be considered a leader? Those are places you might find your answers when it comes to personal branding."

2. Determine where you will get your content to tweet

"Once you have determined your personal brand, the next step is to figure out what content you are going to tweet that fits into your branding strategy. Most of the tweets on Twitter come from three main sources:

▶ "You can retweet people's tweets. I call this going tweet shopping, and it's a great way to find killer content. However, if you are going to establish yourself as a leader in your personal branding niche, you don't want your entire Twitter stream to be retweets. You want to show people that you can find and create content on your own too.

▶ "You can learn how to use curation tools to find good content and then use them on Twitter using cross-platform promotion (CPP).

▶ "You can create your own Twitter content on your blog. My colleague Richard Darell (@Minervity) and I write a minimum of three articles each, every day, seven days a week, for our blog called Bit Rebels. We decided that we wanted to create our own content to tweet. We still retweet a lot, and we still tweet content from other sites that we find. However, the majority of our content we create ourselves. We used Twitter as a springboard for our blog which launched in June 2009. We write geeky content, which fits our personal branding objectives and now have between 2 million and 4 million visitors on our site each month."

One of the keys to success on Twitter is being consistent, so it's important to determine where exactly your tweets will come from, so you will have a consistent supply of content to send out to your followers. And don't forget to use the four types of tweet introduced in Chapter 5.

3. Invite people to see the real you

"Use every opportunity Twitter gives you to invite people to see you as a real person and get to know you.

For people to like, trust, and connect with your personal brand, they have to be able to see you as a human being. Twitter gives each of us several opportunities to promote ourselves, yet so few people take advantage of them. If you are promoting your personal brand, be sure to fill out your complete Twitter bio, keeping it in sync with your brand message.

"This includes a personal profile picture (headshots work well), a completely-filled-out bio that describes you, a link to your blog or other site, and a location. If you travel a lot and want to put 'worldwide' for your location, that is fine. People put some funny things in that space, but just don't leave it blank. Leaving any aspect of your Twitter bio blank sends a message that you were too lazy to complete it.

"Twitter also gives you the opportunity to jazz up your Twitter background with graphics. There are many websites you can go to which offer free Twitter backgrounds, or of course, you can use a personal photograph or create one of your own."

4. Be likable, be yourself, and engage

"Once you've determined your personal brand message, you've figured out where you are going to get your content to tweet, and you've completed your Twitter bio, you are ready to go!

"Remember that in addition to great content, you want to engage with people on Twitter and get to know them. I always joke that it's called 'social media' because it's *social*. Again, using the four types of tweet will ensure that you cover all bases and maximize your personal brand message.

"Being on Twitter is like going to a cocktail party, only for this party, you can wear your pajamas instead of a dress. Sometimes people who are new to Twitter get very nervous about how to start a conversation with people and how to get to know them. All you have to remember is to be likable and be yourself. Be the same way as you are offline. You want to be genuine and sincere. If you are doing that, you are doing it right. It's that simple."

5. Don't be bullied

"When Twitter and social media as a whole were very new concepts, there were many people who tried to dictate what was right and what was wrong in social media. In the case of Twitter, I remember those days, and the new people who joined the site did everything the existing people advised because they wanted to 'do it right.'

"Times have changed a lot since then, and there will inevitably be those who, for one reason or another, will decide to criticize or challenge your tweets or style of tweeting. Remember that nobody has the right to tell you that you are tweeting too much or too little. If any person tries to bully you or starts to cramp your Twitter style, you can always unfollow or block that person."

6. Keep it fun

"Because everyone on Twitter follows different people, everyone's Twitter experience is different. Twitter is a very fun, positive, happy place for me. As the saying goes, my friends live in my computer, and I get to talk to them whenever I log into Twitter. If Twitter is not a fun place for you, adjust who you are following. It's that simple. Find someone on Twitter who you like and look at who he or she is following. Check out the bios of those people, and find a new crowd to hang out with. If you follow the right people, Twitter is a blast!"

7. Don't get into rants on your public Twitter stream

"There is nothing that can ruin your personal brand faster on Twitter than having a rant with someone in the stream. It's not worth it. Remember to always keep your cool, and if you need to rant about something, move to a Twitter direct message where it will be kept private.

"I've had people try to bait me into arguments on Twitter, but the way I look at it, I don't want to give that person the satisfaction of showing up on my page, so I just ignore them. If such people continue bothering me, I unfollow them, and in extreme cases I've had to block people. Again, Twitter is like real life in that not everyone will like you. Sooner or later, you may run into bad apples, and when that happens, don't indulge their tantrums but step back and be the better tweeter.

8. Get chatting!

"Twitter chats are made up of groups of people with the same interests who meet on Twitter for one hour either once a week or once a month. They tweet using a specific hashtag, and if you follow along on Twitter search using that hashtag, you can keep up with the conversation and meet a lot of new friends.

"If your personal branding strategy has to do with health, you might want to join the #FitStudio chat. If you are a woman who wants to cyber-meet other strong women on Twitter, you might want to join #BA75chat. If you like country music, the #CMchat (the largest chat on Twitter right now) might be for you. There are hundreds of chats on Twitter, and you can discover them by simply doing a search on Twitter and on Google."

9. Remember that on Twitter, you have to give before you receive

"This golden rule is alive and well on Twitter, and has been since the beginning. If you want to be recognized on Twitter as a leader and if you want your personal brand to grow, it's important to give before you will receive. If you want more retweets, retweet others. If you want more help figuring things out, help others with things you know how to do. If you want more people to engage with you and tweet you, you have to engage with others and tweet them first.

"The most important thing is to never give up. Twitter is huge and can be an intimidating platform for newbies. It might take a little time to get your personal brand noticed by others. If you are genuine and consistent, though, it is only a matter of time until it all clicks for you!"

10. Overcome Twitter burnout

"I've had social media burnout before, and I can assure you that it's a very real feeling. It's tough because, if you are like me and if the majority of your friends are online, you miss them terribly when you are offline. However, if you are online 24/7, eventually your mental and physical state may start requiring more time offline.

"There are things I've done to overcome that Twitter burnout feeling, including eating meals away from my computer, keeping in touch with phone friends, and remembering that it's all about balance.

Diana Adams' Favorite Twitter Tools

"I've used too many Twitter tools over the years to even count," Diana tells me. "I used Twitter.com for the first month I was on Twitter, and then I quickly learned how important it is to filter tweets from specific people, as it cuts down on the noise. According to a Twitter tool I checked out today for the first time, I have more than 179,000 tweets that I would see every day if I looked at my Twitter stream all day long. That is a lot of tweets! So, I definitely rely on my tools to help streamline things a bit.

"Over the years, I've used TweetDeck, TweetCaster, HootSuite, Seesmic, CoTweet, Pluggio, Echofon, and many more. Most people I know have experimented with different tools.

TweetChat # Enter hashtag to follov [Go »] [Sign In]

How to use TweetChat

1

Sign in to TweetChat.

Signup with Twitter if you don't have an account.

Our login securely authenticates you with Twitter. Once authenticated, you will be returned directly to TweetChat.

If you ever want to sign in as a different user, sign out at Twitter and return to TweetChat.

2

Choose hashtag to follow.

Hashtags identify specific topics and those hashtags allow TweetChat to connect you with people talking about similar things.

TweetChat helps put your blinders on to the Twitter-sphere while you monitor and chat about one topic.

Choosing a hashtag directs you to a TweetChat room.

3

Converse in real-time.

Each tweet automatically gets the hashtag added and the room auto-updates.

You can use the "User Control" area to feature people you like or to block spammers.

"Smart pausing" has been added so when you scroll down the page, it will not refresh, helping you avoid replying to the wrong person.

Follow us on Twitter today: @TweetChat | Privacy Policy

FIGURE 13-6

Diana uses tool such as TweetChat to help her keep in touch with her many followers.

"First of all, as you grow your personal brand and your followers on Twitter, your needs change. A tool or app that worked before suddenly might not be fulfilling your needs anymore. Also, some of these apps (like a lot of Twitter tools) work exceptionally well but only until you reach a certain number of people that you follow. I don't follow everyone back, but I do follow most people back. As a result, I'm following more than 62,000 people. A lot of Twitter tools get wonky when they have to manage that many people.

"So, I'm on an ever-changing quest to find the perfect tool, and so far I haven't found it. Right now I'm using TweetDeck on my iPhone and my laptop, but will most likely be changing soon.

"Some other more general Twitter tools to try are ManageFlitter (to manage who you follow, to link Google+ to Twitter, and to find out who unfollowed you), Tweepi (to unfollow inactive Twitter accounts), Buffer (to efficiently schedule tweets), TweetChat [shown in Figure 13-6] to easily participate in Twitter chats without getting overwhelmed, TweetReach (to see how far a particular tweet traveled), TwitterCounter (to get a report and graph of your general Twitter stats), and — I could go on and on.

"There are more than 70,000 Twitter apps and probably just as many Twitter tools available for you to try out. Most of them are cheeky and fun, but some are really powerful!"

A Life-Changing Personal Brand Experience

For some people, building a personal brand on Twitter can seem like a daunting task. Diana makes it look simple but acknowledges, "There are so many details to think about, and if you aren't careful, it might even start to feel like a chore. Remember to keep it fun. The best personal brands on Twitter were built from that foundation. Keep it simple, and keep it human.

"I've made connections on Twitter that are invaluable, and I've had once-in-a-lifetime experiences that I would have never been able to have if it weren't for Twitter. For example, because I met @Lotay on Twitter, I was invited to fly to Shanghai for a Black Card Circle charity event. It was an experience that changed my life and my view of the world [see Figure 13-7].

FIGURE 13-7

Diana was invited by fellow tweeter @Lotay to attend a Black Card Circle charity in Shanghai.

"Another example of the incredible connections I've made is the Badass Twitter Women [#BA75] group. Along with @HowellMarketing, I wrote an article on Bit Rebels about the 75 most bad-ass women on Twitter. I had no idea when I wrote it of the impact it would make. That article has gone viral many times over, and the sisterhood and bond between all the women in it is something we all cherish. It's a bond that will last forever."

Diana believes that Twitter is so much more than just another social network. "Sure, it's exciting to get a tweet from a celebrity every once in a while, and a lot of people join the site hoping for that experience, but for me, it's not about that at all. Twitter is a site that has changed the lives of so many ordinary people like you and me, and the opportunities there are endless. Don't be afraid. Dive in and take advantage of it all. It's right there waiting for you!"

"The best path to success is your own!"

@AmitV_Tweets

14

Social Media Entrepreneur at 17

To have founded three successful companies is quite an achievement. To have founded them all by the age of 17 is nothing short of phenomenal, and that's the best word with which to describe Amit Verma (@AmitV_Tweets).

This brilliant young entrepreneur has a wise head on his young shoulders, something that comes across clearly in his personal brand message. Amit built a strong personal brand on Twitter and credits much of his companies' successes to Twitter. He first learned of Twitter as a young schoolboy, when it was officially launched back in 2006, but remembers being "too busy concentrating on my studies to sign up." His first priority back then, he remembers, was to "make my parents proud," which they certainly were when he finally graduated from high school with exceptional grades.

Later, Amit's love of technology led him to become an avid reader of technology and gadget-related articles, and it led him back to Twitter once more. He recalls, "I'm very much a gadget freak and love to discover info about them. It was while watching a television show on gadgets Twitter was mentioned again, and I suddenly felt drawn to the excitement of the platform and what I felt it could offer me in terms of meeting others with interests similar to mine."

Amit signed up and created an account on Twitter (see Figure 14-1). It was a life-changing moment for him: "I decided to create my Twitter account on my birthday and it turned out to be the best gift I could have possibly given myself. Twitter is incredibly popular, the growth rate is exponential, and it's here to stay. There are thousands and thousands of great people to network and socialize with on the platform, and suddenly I could reach them all."

Establishing Brand Visibility

Amit believes that what you tweet can help shape your brand on Twitter. For example, if you regularly help others with business ideas, you will soon become

Amit Verma

@AmitV_Tweets FOLLOWS YOU

*CEO and Founder of @ModernLifeBlogs & @ModernLifePix Loves
Technology, Quotes, Health Topics, Music, Photography & Spreading
Love & Smiles :-)*

India · http://www.modernlifeblogs.com

FIGURE 14-1

Amit Verma has found early personal branding success through Twitter. His Twitter profile and bio perfectly reflect his innovative personal brand.

known as the business ideas go-to person. Humorous individuals will be known as fun and will gain followers who appreciate their sense of humor. Twitter may bring an impact to your brand based on the human qualities that are given out through your tweets every day.

Amit believes it's also important to choose your content wisely because, once you tweet, it will be out there for others to find forever, "As a tweeter, you are going to be visible, so make sure you do it in the right way and to the right group of people and influencers."

Using cross-platform promotion (CPP) effectively is another way that Amit has successfully built his personal brand using Twitter. He uses the platform to link to his website, blog, and application platforms as part of his daily Twitter show schedule (see Figure 14-2).

"If you want to build your brand, it will be far more effective if you expand your visibility across multiple platforms," Amit explains. "Creating a web presence is a good start. Build a blog and update it frequently. Make sure that you create eye-catching tweets to link to them on a daily basis and to keep your followers entertained. My blog, ModernLifeBlogs. com [see Figure 14-3], is about inspiration, technology, social media, and personal growth, so my tweets are all geared around these topics and tied into the blog through regular links."

Amit doesn't just stay behind the keyboard but plays a regular role in industry events that further boosts his personal brand and showcases his early achievements. "It is easier to establish trust if you directly meet with individuals. If early brand visibility is important to you, you may want to combine your online presence with real-life attendance at industry events. Talk to real people. This kind of interaction will often lead to many great things in the future, and it's a great way to create a buzz about your brand on Twitter prior to an event."

Amit Verma
@AmitV_Tweets

 Following

How To Be Productive & Stress Free At The Same
Time bit.ly/K1NNFK

Reply   Retweet   Favorite   Buffer

FIGURE 14-2

Amit links his tweets to new and popular blog posts.

Amit recommends creating a Twitter background that resembles the colors, format, and logo from your personal or corporate website: "When you create your background, add information that isn't covered in your Twitter profile, such as pointers to more websites or information about products or services you sell. If you're trying to build a strong personal brand, focus your Twitter handle, profile picture, and bio information 100 percent on you, instead of your company."

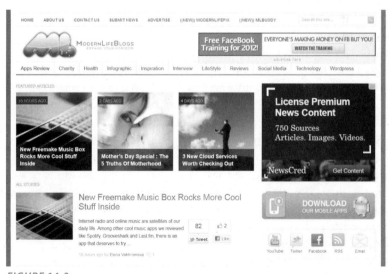

FIGURE 14-3

Amit cofounded the highly successful ModernLifeBlogs, whose posts have been shared more than 500,000 times.

Amit Verma's Golden Rules to Personal Branding Success

Amit has eight best practices for successful personal branding.

1. Review your Twitter activity

"Begin each day by checking your Twitter streams for mentions and direct messages and to establish what your followers are talking and tweeting about. Use the four types of tweets to respond, thank, RT, engage, and react accordingly. Depending on level of engagement, reacting can take up to an hour each day, but it's time well spent.

"Pay particular attention to Twitter posts from key influencers in your fields of interest and follow the people they follow. Join discussions and participate in Twitter chats. If they're interesting enough, you'll find many other like-minded people to follow on Twitter and gain additional followers as a result."

2. Promote your blog posts

"Twitter is a great tool for promoting your blog and other posts you may find interesting. Sharing through effective cross-platform promotion (CPP) is a key factor in my personal branding success. I use my afternoons to update my blog, which includes writing new posts, scheduling others, and checking the drafts of any pending posts. After this, I tweet my latest post with a great headline to grab attention and a link to the post itself. I also send the tweet as a direct message to key influencers who can help spread the news about it. I make time to respond to any comments both on the blog itself and via Twitter throughout the day.

"It's great to be able to have the opportunity through Twitter to ask for people's reactions about my posts, and I also welcome interesting guests posts [see Figure 14-4]. Whenever possible, I try to solve problems from readers who may want additional information about topics I have covered on my blog."

3. Sharing is caring

"I can't reiterate enough just how important engagement and sharing are for personal branding success on Twitter. When my working

Amit Verma
@AmitV_Tweets

Guest Post: Change of Pace by Sofia Essen
goo.gl/uQCL9 via @osvme

← Reply ⇄ Retweet ★ Favorite ≋ Buffer

FIGURE 14-4

Amit is always happy to feature interesting guest posts on his blog.

day is done, I return to Twitter to socialize and share my tweets and my thanks for any mentions or retweets given to me [see Figure 14-5]. It's a very rewarding time and is always a great reminder of how much friendship and support I have on the platform."

4. Schedule tweets during peak times

"I use scheduling tools such as Buffer [see Figure 14-6] to ensure that my tweets go out at optimum times throughout the day. The most effective U.S. times I have noticed are between 7:00 and 9:00 a.m. CST, 12:00 p,m. CST, and between 7:00 and 9:00 p.m. EST."

5. Build your social media presence with tweet chats

"Your presence on Twitter is wonderfully effective as a source of traffic for your blog or website. In addition, the contacts you build on Twitter help

Amit Verma
@AmitV_Tweets

Welcome bro. How are you? RT @brasonja: @AmitV_Tweets Thanks bro, have a great weekend!

← Reply ⇄ Retweet ★ Favorite ≋ Buffer

FIGURE 14-5

Amit enjoys time on Twitter catching up with friends and socializing with new followers.

FIGURE 14-6

Amit schedules many of his daily tweets using tools like Buffer.

in the real world, as well as the interaction on Twitter, invariably give way to organized meetings for people who interact regularly."

6. Connect with people irrespective of their geographic location

"Geographic location and time zone shouldn't be an obstacle to interaction on Twitter. Get to know people from around the world and connect through shared interests."

7. Join in the hype around a trending topic

"Tweets with hashtags give shape to a trending topic on Twitter. As more people tweet on a particular trending topic, Twitter gets its own little revolution that shapes people's opinions and unites them. Be a part of it!"

8. Use a great Twitter client

"The new Twitter has a great interface but for me, the Twitter client of choice is TweetDeck [see Figure 14-7]. It's a free app that brings more

FIGURE 14-7

TweetDeck is Amit's Twitter client of choice and one that he uses every day.

flexibility and insight to power users and people serious about building a personal brand. TweetDeck allows you to arrange your feeds in customizable columns. You can focus on what really matters by using its powerful filters.

"Like Buffer, TweetDeck allows you to schedule your Tweets to suit your audience's time zones. You can monitor and manage unlimited Twitter accounts and you can stay up to date with customizable notification alerts for new tweets. I use TweetDeck every day and wouldn't be without it."

The Future

Amit's personal branding success story is truly inspirational. He has not only embraced Twitter as a social tool but also as a powerhouse of knowledge and connections that he uses to promote and expand each of his business ventures.

His entrepreneurial empire is continuing to grow, with new applications in the pipeline that he's gearing up to tweet about. Look for news of them in a Twitter stream near you!

"No matter how smart or talented you are, you won't get results without doing the work!"

@AskAaronLee

15

Meet the Twitter Ninja

Another young success story is that of Aaron Lee (@AskAaronLee), who is a social media manager, entrepreneur, and as he likes to call himself "an acclaimed ninja hailing from Malaysia."

Aaron's clear talent in social media management, coupled with his sincere and open personal brand (see his bio in Figure 15-1), has seen his following on Twitter and many other social media platforms soar over the past two years.

Aaron's work has been featured on prominent sites such as the Huffington Post and iStrategyConference.com, in which he contributes weekly as a blogger. He has also been listed as one of the top social media personalities on Sprout Social Insights Wall of Fame (see Figure 15-2).

Aaron is the social ninja behind Binkd, a social media marketing platform for promotions, including contests, customer rewards, and incentive programs (see Figure 15-3). This accomplished young man has been featured on numerous blogs and websites, as well as appearing in local newspapers such as the *Star Malaysia* and *Kosmo Malaysia*.

Aaron possesses a genuine love for helping people, something that has seen him rank Number 4 in the Top 100 Small Business Experts to Follow on Twitter (see Figure 15-4).

Aaron Lee
@AskAaronLee FOLLOWS YOU
Small business owner with a huge vision, Average Joe who loves social media more than his coffee (I really love coffee!!), Social Media Consultant to pay bills
Malaysia   http://AskAaronLee.com

Following 🔽

64,460 TWEETS
130,073 FOLLOWING
317,017 FOLLOWERS

FIGURE 15-1

Aaron Lee's Twitter bio shows both his work ethic and his humor.

About Aaron Lee

FIGURE 15-2

Aaron has been listed in Sprout Social Insights Wall of Fame.

FIGURE 15-3

Aaron is the social ninja behind Binkd social media promotions and rewards.

February 2012 Top 100 Small Business Experts to Follow on Twitter

#1) @Forbes - Forbes (Up from #3)

#2) @SteveCase - Steve Case (Up from #7)

#3) @Inc - Inc.

#4) @AskAaronLee - Aaron Lee (Up from #5)

#5) @TheoPaphitis - Theo Paphitis (Up from #18)

FIGURE 15-4

Aaron is listed as Number 4 in the Top 100 Small Business Experts to Follow on Twitter.

He possesses the spirit of a true entrepreneur, a facet that has recently led him to team with his girlfriend Jin Lee as a cofounder of Leneys, an independent women's apparel company, shown in Figure 15-5.

FIGURE 15-5

Aaron is the cofounder of popular online fashion company Leneys, along with his girlfriend Jin Lee, after whom the business is named.

Searching for Possibilities

Aaron's personal branding success story began back in 2008. He recalls, "It was the holidays and I didn't want to look for a part-time job, so I searched for alternative ways to make additional income. While at the bookstore one day, I stumbled upon a book about Internet marketing and, after browsing through the first few pages, I was immediately hooked. I read about the possibilities to make income through blogs and other Internet media, so I started a blog about coffee and was blogging throughout my time in the university."

Because Aaron needed to build traffic to his blog, he looked for ways to get it ranked higher on Google. Doing so took a lot of time and expertise, so he was curious to discover other ways of bringing more attention to his blog. "I remember coming across an article about how Twitter could help me link my blog to other people, and I believed that this was a good idea. I registered in March 2009. At the time, Ashton Kutcher and CNN were battling each other to be the first to get to 1 million followers. Ashton won."

At first, Aaron didn't get what Twitter was about. He did, however, notice that some people were using the platform like a diary: sharing their to-do lists, what they just ate, and what they were going to do. So he started to post his own diary-style tweets about his daily life. "I posted tweets like 'going to class' or 'writing a blog post now,' and a follower responded to my tweets asking me what my blog post was about. After finishing the post, I sent him the link to my blog and he told me that he loved the article. It wowed me!"

Aaron knew that he had stumbled onto something special. He remembers the thrill of that first memorable connection: "Twitter wasn't like other social networking sites where you are limited to engaging with friends. With Twitter, I am able to connect with just about anyone on earth. Engagement was fun and quick, and I felt like I was in a massive online chat room. It was also easy for me to stay connected to people I liked, as all I needed to do was follow them, no friend requests needed. I'm still connected to some of the people I knew back then, and we've been friends ever since."

Lessons Learned

After using Twitter for a while, and having fewer than 100 followers at that time, Aaron realized that he had only scratched the surface of what Twitter was capable of doing for his personal brand. "I hadn't been using it at its highest potential. I wanted to know everything about it, so I began reading articles about how to grow my followers. Because Twitter was so new and fresh at that time, there wasn't much information, and it was difficult to tell what the best way to move forward was."

Aaron applied some of the techniques mentioned in blogs at the time, such as randomly following people and following everyone back. This proved to be a huge mistake because, although the number of his followers grew, he was clearly following a lot of spammers and bots, too.

"I used to see great tweets from people that mattered, but now all I was seeing were spam tweets about tooth whitening and forex trading. It was an important lesson for me. Because Twitter didn't have listing options at the time, it was hard to follow meaningful conversations, and I regretted not being able to connect more with the great personalities I had met earlier."

Luckily enough, Twitter's list option was launched at the end of 2009 and Aaron was able to vastly improve the way he managed his followers. "I realized that I needed to restructure the way I was growing my profile, so I searched for top social media blogs, followed the most influential people in social media, followed who they were talking to, and who was talking to them. I knew that I needed to know them and I needed them to know me. I responded to tweets, I left comments on their blogs, and I did everything I had to do to get noticed."

Aaron learned that meaningful interaction and communication were the key to growing a valuable Twitter following.

As Aaron begun sharing information that he'd learned from blogs and other websites, his followers started sharing and retweeting his tweets. He even had people who were keen to ask him questions, as his handle is @AskAaronLee.

He remembers one of the weirdest questions asked was "What is the meaning of life?" "After finding myself repeatedly answering a couple of similar questions about Twitter, I decided to start writing through my blog on January 1, 2010. I wanted to share my experiences with not only my followers but also with people who are looking for it outside of Twitter. From that moment onward, my brand was slowly built to what it is today."

A Permanent Twitter Connection

Twitter has now become a major part of Aaron's life and, as such, a part of his personal brand. "It is with me 24/7," he says. "I can't remember the last time I've not used it. Ever since I started using Twitter in 2009, I am always connected to it.

"Every morning, Twitter is one of the first things I check. I'll respond to the first couple tweets before I even get out of my bed. I just love the level of engagement I get with people, and I find that I am able to learn so much from so many people around the world. It relaxes me."

This psychological state of relaxation connected to the feeling of emotional engagement through Twitter is widely acknowledged as one of the reasons for its tremendous success. In fact, the level of engagement on Twitter can't be compared to other networks, as it is faster and far more personal. Aaron believes that "Facebook and Google+ are great, but Twitter is more personal because every tweet or response in your stream makes an instant emotional connection and feels only for you."

Aaron also says that he finds it harder to stand out on sites like Facebook and Google+. "When I respond to a wall post or status update, my messages gets mixed with other conversations. But on Twitter, people notice my tweets because they get to view them individually."

When it comes to creating content on Twitter, Aaron is constantly sharing what he finds interesting and what he feels adds value to others. "It could be a serious-looking article about life, a simple and cheerful infographic, or materials that would make people laugh and brighten their day. Whatever I share, I want it to be meaningful."

The Benefits of Asking Questions

Aaron believes that the best type of communication and engagement comes from asking questions, adding, "I ask lots of them on Twitter." He finds that questions asked on Twitter generate a far greater response than when posted on other platforms (see an example in Figure 15-6).

@AskAaronLee
Aaron Lee

How many hours are you
connected to the internet a day?
No cheating! :)

31 minutes ago via CoTweet

☆ Favorite ↻ Reply 🗑 Delete

replies ↓

sno_buny Lovyst Going
good ? - probly 2 many! lol rt @AskAaronLee
How many hours are you connected to the
internet a day? No cheating! :)
19 minutes ago

Arien1976 Arien Westmaas
@AskAaronLee - 24 hours
23 minutes ago

FIGURE 15-6

Aaron has discovered that asking questions is a great way to connect and to create a buzz.

"I noticed that when I ask people to choose between two options, it creates great engagement and buzz. One of the best questions I've asked was 'Which cake would you choose: chocolate or cheesecake?' In minutes I had hundreds of responses and some who even cheekily answered 'chocolate cheesecake,' which was hilarious because I wouldn't have thought of it."

Aaron Lee's Golden Rules for Personal Branding Success

Aaron has ten best practices for successful personal branding.

1. Have a great profile photo

"One mistake that most newbies make is not having a profile photo up prior to sending out tweets. That is the worst possible way to start on Twitter as it makes them seem like a spammer. People don't want to talk to a faceless profile or that mysterious Twitter egg.

"Users need to understand that their profile photo is their personal brand on Twitter and all other social networking sites. People remember profile photos even more than they remember usernames."

2. Get a good username

"Your username on Twitter is your personal brand identity. The best tip I would give is to go for your own name. If it is taken, try adding words that represent what you do or what you want your brand to be. Because I didn't know what I wanted my branding to be when I got started, I used @AskAaronLee. It is personal because it still has my name in it, it is easy to brand because it is simple, and the .com domain name was available, too.

"I don't recommend people use a numeric username like @ Aaron1202 because names like this are hard to remember, which is bad for branding."

3. Fill up your bio

"Another mistake that many new Twitter users make is not taking advantage of their bio. Many people on Twitter will check out your bio before deciding whether to follow you or not. I would advise not to fill your bio with too many keywords but to keep the meaning real and true to your brand message."

Here's a good bio: "Chieftain of the social web's most unique blog, {grow}. Consultant, college professor, author of Return On Influence and Tao of Twitter. Social Media Bouncer. @MarkWSchaefer"

Here's a bad bio: "Social Media | Blogger | Facebook | Twitter | Linkedin"

4. Follow people based on interest first

"To grow a brand on Twitter, you need followers. Otherwise, you'll feel like a crazy person talking to yourself. Start by following the top people in your industry first. Follow people who are talking to them, and follow who they are talking to. You need to be part of that group and you need people in that group to know you."

5. Become an expert

"If you want to brand yourself well on Twitter, you need to be an expert on a particular topic. When I started out, most of my tweets were asking for advice about Twitter because I wanted to be an expert on that topic. You need to be the guy that people think about when they are searching for a particular topic."

6. Share other people's content

"Most users start by sharing their content to build traffic. Although the logic of branding is to let people know of your presence, I believe that sharing too much of your own content is the wrong way start branding. You need to share other people's content so they will notice you by making sure that you add their Twitter usernames in your tweets. The best formula is to have a consistent ratio. For example, for every one tweet about your brand, share eight tweets about other people's content. You don't like meeting people who only talk about themselves, so start by letting people know that you are willing to listen and share."

7. Participate

"What makes Twitter great? The conversation. Twitter is a great place to not only build relationships but create engagement. Yes, you will need to share content; however, creating conversations is equally important. You can tweet to the people in your industry, respond to tweets they post, answer any questions they ask, or even ask them questions. The key is to participate."

8. Be consistent

"Every user needs to develop a consistent habit on Twitter when it comes to tweeting, responding to other tweets, and most important, showing up on Twitter. Many newbies use Twitter only for a couple of weeks, give up, and say that it doesn't work. You'll only stay in shape if you eat healthy and exercise constantly, and it is the same when it comes to Twitter. For your account to be healthy, you need to spend time and effort on it."

9. Help others

To grow a strong brand, help others. To find out what people need help in, you can search on Twitter and find the questions people are asking. Find questions that nobody else might be answering. A good example is Gary Vaynerchuck (@garyvee), who started out on Twitter by searching for those asking questions about wine and answering all of them."

10. Have fun

"Last, just have fun as you go along. If you aren't having fun, you won't enjoy using Twitter and you won't stay the course, which is vital for personal brand success."

Aaron Lee's Favorite Twitter Tools

As with all the personal branding superstars in Part Four, I asked Aaron what tools he finds the most valuable in managing his Twitter presence.

"I tend to get this question a lot," he remarked. "People want to know what the best tool to use is. My answer will always be that the best tool is right in front of them and it's free. It's called Twitter.com. What not many people know is that they are able to do almost everything on Twitter itself. The website comes with a great search tool; you can search for users to follow or even track conversations about a particular topic. I still use the search tool even though I have seen and tested many other external tools for Twitter. I find that the most important tool will always be Twitter itself, because Twitter wasn't built to be managed by external tools, Twitter was built to be self-sustainable. I believe that every user should get to know the functionality of Twitter.com before they decide if an external tool is required to manage their account."

Aaron also believes that too much time is spent on finding the right tools to manage Twitter instead of focusing on the real magic of Twitter itself. Having said that, Aaron acknowledges that there are tools that help to ease work on Twitter. He believes the best fit ultimately depends on what users of Twitter want to achieve. Aaron's personal favorite is CoTweet (see Figure 15-7). "I have tried and tested many tools, but one

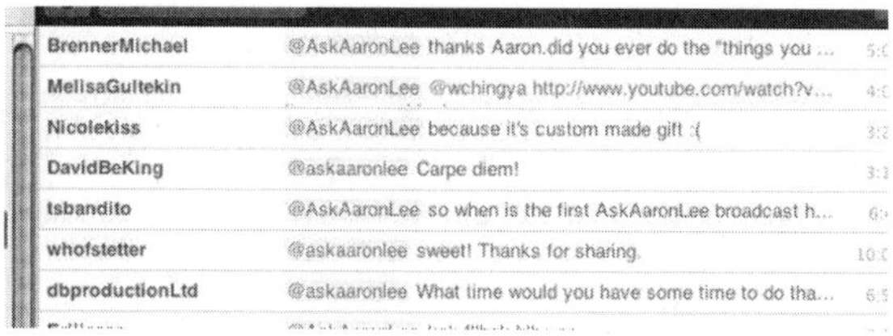

BrennerMichael	@AskAaronLee thanks Aaron,did you ever do the "things you ...	5:(
MelisaGultekin	@AskAaronLee @wchingya http://www.youtube.com/watch?v...	4:(
Nicolekiss	@AskAaronLee because it's custom made gift :(	3:2
DavidBeKing	@askaaronlee Carpe diem!	3:1
tsbandito	@AskAaronLee so when is the first AskAaronLee broadcast h...	6:
whofstetter	@askaaronlee sweet! Thanks for sharing.	10:(
dbproductionLtd	@askaaronlee What time would you have some time to do tha...	6:5

FIGURE 15-7

CoTweet's unique features help Aaron focus on the quality of his engagement.

that got me to continue using it even today is CoTweet. I've been a fan of CoTweet since I started using it in 2010.

"What CoTweet does that many other tools aren't able to do is to group my replies. As my Twitter stream becomes busy with retweets and group chats, I might want to focus on other tweets that were sent directly to me prior to a question. CoTweet allows me to separate the retweets and the direct @askaaronlee replies. This helps me to focus on separate sessions of conversations and helps me improve the quality of my engagement."

The Voice of Your Brand

Aaron always tells people "my blog is my thoughts and Twitter is my voice."

Aaron uses cross-platform promotion (CPP) to unite the message of his blog with his personal brand growth using Twitter. "I was able to grow a strong brand on Twitter because I had a blog. AskAaronLee.com helped give people tips and advice about Twitter, and people appreciated it. My blog enables me to answer more questions and by doing so it indirectly helped me to grow a strong personal brand on Twitter too [see Figure 15-8]. Not only was I able to share my thoughts, I was able to share my expertise and what I know about Twitter. AskAaronLee.com has helped my branding so much that I landed a job in an agency even before graduating from university."

Aaron's personal brand voice continues to grow through his adaptive and insightful use of Twitter as a platform to echo his talents and vision. He is one of those early Twitter adopters who just had an instinctive knowledge of the power of the platform, perhaps even before the developers themselves.

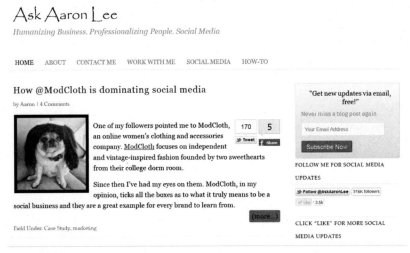

FIGURE 15-8

Aaron's blog (AskAaronLee.com) is a great example of using cross-platform promotion (CPP) to promote a personal brand.

His willingness to push the boundaries of what Twitter can provide in personal brand value is a truly inspirational story.

"It's a big world out there. It would be a shame not to experience it :) #travel"

@earthXplorer

16

Tweeting around the World

Video producer and long-time travel blogger JD Andrews (@earthXplorer, as he is known by his thousands of Twitter followers and as shown in his bio in Figure 16-1), has visited more than 83 countries across all seven continents, and always with a camera in hand.

JD recently won a Shorty Award (the Oscar of Twitter awards, by the way) for travel, as shown in Figure 16-2, and is acknowledged as not only a travel and production expert but as an all-around nice guy with a huge loyal Twitter following.

JD was born and raised on a mountain in Colorado, moved to the desert of Arizona, then spent 11 years at sea traveling the world. His job was video production, but along the way he also fell in love with photography. To date, JD has spent more than 20 years traveling around the globe, shooting and editing travel and tourism videos for various cruise lines, airlines, and tourist boards.

These projects have presented JD with once-in-a-lifetime experiences and the chance to see the amazing world we live in. He has written for various travel magazines, as well as blog posts for *National Geographic* and BBC Travel and was featured on Huffington Post Travel and AOL Travel (see Figure 16-3).

JD Andrews
@earthXplorer FOLLOWS YOU
+World Traveler, Dad, 3xEmmy winner, Video, Adventure, Photographer, ♥dogs, Sharing & Caring, Travel & Social Media, I tweet a lot! https://vimeo.com/37989027
Miami, Fl. USA   http://www.earthxplorer.com

Following 👤▾

91,665 TWEETS
75,362 FOLLOWING
88,706 FOLLOWERS

FIGURE 16-1

The well-known profile photo and bio of JD Andrews reflects his warmth and passion for travel.

FIGURE 16-2

JD was winner of the Shorty Award for travel in 2011.

FIGURE 16-3

JD has been featured worldwide in media such as the BBC (shown here) and Lonely Planet.

FIGURE 16-4

JD is a producer and cohost of GoingSocialTV, which he founded in 2010.

JD is the host and producer of GoingSocialTV, which features regular interviews with social media leaders and top corporations (see Figure 16-4).

An Early Adopter

JD joined Twitter in July 2007 and fondly recalls his first experience of the platform. "I'm what many refer to as an early adopter. That's a nice way of saying 'nerd boy,' which means I consume a lot of information from geeky blogs and podcasts.

"It was back in 2007 that I first heard of this new way to send text messages on the Internet called Twitter. So I quickly joined, because the other geeks had, all the while not knowing what it was or how I would use it. I was confused by the 140-character limitation and how you find other people to tweet with. I did love the idea of communicating with people

JD Andrews
@earthXplorer

Following ●▾

Good Morning from Barcelona! Getting ready for the #catalunyaexperience :-)

↩ Reply ⇄ Retweet ★ Favorite ⧩ Buffer

FIGURE 16-5

JD loves being able to communicate in real time with followers around the world.

from all over the world, asking questions and getting a tremendous range of responses. Simply typing 'good morning' and seeing tweets from people that I would never have known without this new thing in social media" (see Figure 16-5).

As one of the early adopters of Twitter, JD had an opportunity to play a part in how it was being used and ultimately how it would evolve. He remembers, "Celebrities, companies, and brands had not yet discovered Twitter. Most were happy to be on Facebook and showed no interest in another new social media platform.

"Back then, there were no groups, lists, or even a standard to retweet. I remember the day, as a community, we were discussing how to properly retweet someone. We all understood the power of Twitter is sharing and needed to ensure the original author of the tweet was recognized. We were using 'Re-Tweet,' but decided that it took too many characters. Some ideas included using 'RTweet' or the recycle symbol, but finally everyone agreed on simply using 'RT.'"

Branding Lessons Learned along the Way

JD entered a steep learning curve when he adopted Twitter as a new means of social networking. Over time, it became far more than that to him, something very personal and deeply rooted in his brand. But with this realization came the knowledge that, with hindsight, there were things he might have done differently.

'Put the orange guy back!'

"When I set up my Twitter account, I never thought of it as my brand or what I should add to my profile. I just found a photo from an Alaska trip, put it up there and, five years later, it's considered my brand. I have tried to change my profile photo, but every time I do my Twitter friends tell me to 'put the orange guy back!' It's easy to see and recognize as @earthXplorer. But if I had known that photo was going to be my brand, I would have picked a different one."

Becoming categorized

"Slowly, just being on Twitter wasn't enough. People were starting to categorize everyone, so instead of @earthXplorer being a dog-loving dad who enjoys art, music, movies, Apple products, photography, and cool gadgets, and who's a kinda geeky guy who loves to travel and does video production for a living, I was put in the travel category. This is fine, but I miss the days where we all just communicated and shared, not limiting who you followed or shared with due to their category."

On oversharing and direct messages

"As stated in my Twitter profile, I tweet a lot ☺. I like to over-share, my travels, random thoughts, photos, quotes, and any trivia that I think is fun. I spend most of my day on Twitter, but I never let it interrupt or change what I am doing; it just becomes a part of it. I hear so many people say, 'I just don't have time for Twitter.' Well, in answer to that, I'd have to say that it takes as much time as you want to give it.

"I try to respond to any tweet that asks a direct question — if it's not a spam account — and I like to comment on tweets that I find interesting. I used to answer every single DM [direct message] I received, but nowadays there is just way too much spam, making DMs almost useless" (see Figure 16-6).

JD Andrews
@earthXplorer

 Following

I just want ONE DM that reads "Hello this user is saying great things about you..." #2MuchSpam

← Reply ⭤ Retweet ★ Favorite ⧂ Buffer

FIGURE 16-6

JD finds direct messages almost useless these days, due to the amount of spam he receives.

JD Andrews' Golden Rules for Personal Branding Success

As with all the personal branding success stories in Part Four, I wanted to glean some valuable Twitter tips from JD that you can put into practice right away. Here are his top ten pointers:

1. Find your voice

"Are you a character? Funny, silly, snarky, cheeky, mean, or just plain nice? Whatever your character, let it shine in your Twitter voice."

2. Follow people that you believe are interesting

"They'll be plenty of suggestions, of course, from Twitter itself and from others on the platform, but let your own interests and preferences ultimately be your guide to who you choose to follow. Don't be swayed by others. Remember that you're the best judge of what appeals to you."

3. Keep active

"Try to keep your account active, even if you only tweet once a day. That way, people know you are participating and are more likely to follow you."

4. Put away the megaphone and start listening

"Twitter has broken the rules of traditional forms of marketing. It's very much a two-way conversation, a dialog as opposed to a monolog form of communication. It's a relationship-based networking tool that goes far beyond the blanket posting mediums of the past. This is a fact that you need to fully take on board and embrace to effectively build your personal brand on Twitter."

5. Don't make your profile picture an afterthought

Make sure you get your photo on your profile as soon as possible. People rarely follow the egg. But, as I've already mentioned, make sure you pick the right photo to reflect your personal brand. Mine has stuck in the mind of my followers and as a result can't be changed now. But, with hindsight, I'd have picked a different photo from the beginning."

6. Do not use an auto-DM — nope, never!

"Enough said!"

7. Be sweet and retweet

"It's courtesy to show respect for others on Twitter. I like to say, 'A tweets life is short and sweet, so if you enjoy, please retweet." Show your appreciation for information, links, photos, and tips that you find interesting and that add value to you and your personal brand."

8. Use the SITE method of tweeting

"Getting the right mix of tweets is crucial to getting your personal brand message across effectively, so I'm always careful to ensure I'm using the four types of tweet defined by @grattongirl as the SITE method of tweeting. Namely, share, inform, thank, and engage. Getting this balance right will keep your Twitter stream interesting and valuable for your followers."

9. Be helpful

"Twitter provides the opportunity to form relationships with others on a real-time basis that can offer support, friendship, or just a listening ear when needed (albeit virtually). Take the time to respond to those people asking questions, looking for help, or just needing to connect. Providing this kind of support can be some of the most rewarding time spent on Twitter."

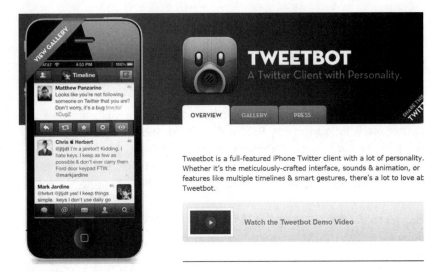

FIGURE 16-7

JD is a fan of Twitter client, Tweetbot, which he uses to read, organize, and send tweets from his iPhone.

10. Be nice!

"Like all communities, Twitter has its grumps, its trolls, and those people who are quite frankly just looking for an argument. Avoid them like the plague and don't get into unfriendly disputes or rants. It's detrimental to your personal brand and a great waste of your valuable time, so my advice is steer well clear and to block any accounts that present themselves as negative forces in your stream."

JD Andrews' Favorite Twitter Tools

JD has always liked the Twitter interface on the web, and back when he started on the platform, there were no tools available, but when he found TweetDeck, HootSuite, and more recently Tweetbot (see Figure 16-7), he was ecstatic.

"Suddenly I didn't have to cut and paste anymore. Retweeting became so much easier, and putting everything in columns really made the Twitter experience so much better. Nowadays, I occasionally use

TweetDeck but primarily stick with HootSuite on my desktop. On my iPhone, I use HootSuite and Tweetbot."

Passion and Luck

JD believes that if you're passionate about what you are doing, it will translate to your personal brand through Twitter. He has mastered the art of being true to himself and to the people that follow him, and he never takes their loyalty for granted.

But he also considers himself extremely fortunate: "I have been so lucky in my Twitter experience, meeting some amazing people online and then in real life and, as I always say, 'Facebook is where you add your friends, Twitter is where you meet them.'"

JD's connections, his wonderful personality, and as he likes to term it, "a big dose of good fortune," have enabled him to travel even more through various Twitter-organized trips, including getting to see one of the last shuttle launches at NASA, exploring Antarctica, and gorilla-trekking in Rwanda. He believes that Twitter has proven to be valuable to him in so many ways and continues to be so: "And now getting my personal brand story published in a book! I would have never guessed that this would be a direct result of signing up to what is a phenomenal social media platform — Twitter."

"Keep smiling friends and see you on the flip side ☺"

@SharonHayes

17

Putting Her Personal Brand in the Pink

Sharon Hayes (@SharonHayes) is a leading Twitter lady who knows exactly where she's going, and it's straight to the top! A successful entrepreneur whose professional yet lovable personal brand is reflected in her Twitter profile (see Figure 17-1), Sharon is widely respected as a businesswoman. All three of her companies specialize in offering marketing-related business-to-business services online, and all have thrived as a result of her personal brand success. As a leader in online marketing, Sharon has had to be ahead of the curve in social media adoption.

Skeptical Beginnings

Sharon's Twitter story began in 2008. She recalls, "Many of my friends and associates were early adopters of social media platforms. In early 2008, I started to receive invitations from people I knew who had joined Twitter. A handful of my clients had also asked about Twitter and my thoughts on how it could be used for business.

"I filed away the invites. I didn't even look at the Twitter website. I knew, conceptually at least, what Twitter was. You could have people opt in to receive your broadcasts of 140 characters. Since the mid-'90s, one of my core areas has been e-mail marketing, and Twitter seemed to be the text/SMS message equivalent.

"But I couldn't see how Twitter could work for business. I likened it to the philosophical question 'If a tree falls in a forest and no one is around to hear it, does it make a sound?' If people aren't actually on Twitter and following a business or brand, what is the point? For Twitter to be a viable marketing method, there had to be a critical mass of users. It would take a massive amount

FIGURE 17-1

Sharon Hayes's vibrant personal brand shines out from her Twitter profile page.

of word of mouth work for it to attract users to make it a sensible route for business users to pursue.

"I eventually created an account on Twitter in September 2008. Initially, I just accepted invites I had already received from people. I attended a business conference in Los Angeles the next month and several contacts I made there had Twitter accounts. Until the end of that year, I used Twitter sporadically for conversational purposes and not much else. Somehow, I got to 500 followers and had maybe 200 or 300 tweets.

"In late December, I discovered one thing about Twitter that changed everything — the retweet! At the time, Twitter had no built-in retweeting function. There was only manual retweeting. I shared a link to one news article, which ended up going viral because of others retweeting it. At the time, people seemed hungry to find new, interesting people to follow. I not only found this one tweet being recirculated, but I also picked up a few dozen new followers the same day.

"A good deal of the online marketing work I've done has been related to viral campaigns. Finding out what retweets could do exposure-wise — I literally felt like I had found the Holy Grail. My enthusiasm for Twitter rapidly kicked in and has stayed with me since."

Taking a Client's Perspective

Sharon's use of Twitter has been what she terms as "an ongoing experiment of sorts." She believes her situation is unique, as although she uses Twitter under her own name, her companies are not tightly linked with her name. She explains, "The average dollar value of a client for me is typically quite high because I deal with larger corporations and organizations. I was more interested in how content flowed to help guide clients than I was for personal business gain.

"There's never really been a point in time where it's been clear from my tweets what exactly I do. I share a variety of information — business, social media, marketing, domains, and motivational — but on the flip side, I also share music, bits of my life, and such. If you look at my tweets, you'll get a blended view of who I am — both business and personal. It's pretty well representative of what my work day and life are like."

In spite of this — or maybe because of this — Sharon has not only built a large following on Twitter but has also gained a significant amount of business.

A Great Example

"One thing to keep in mind when it comes to personal branding today," Sharon exclaims, "is that people are not buying what you sell but are buying you. Showing a likable persona in social media has resulted in a significant amount of referrals for me.

"I'll share an example: One of my core business areas is in domain names. My company, Domainate (see Figure 17-2), helps people find an appropriate domain name for branding or rebranding purposes. Let me tell you, I've worked on marketing in some capacity for companies in just about every industry, and finding the right domain names has to be one of the most difficult services or products with which to target an audience. Without a substantial budget to market, it can be exceptionally difficult to reach people at exactly the right moment they are in need of a new domain name.

"Almost daily, I have a Twitter follower recommend me to someone they know who needs a new domain name. Do they believe my company is the best at this? Maybe not! But they like me and feel confident in directing their friends, associates, and customers to me."

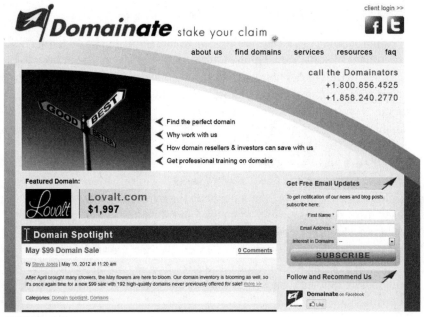

FIGURE 17-2

Sharon's company Domainate has thrived as a result of her Twitter presence.

Lessons Learned

If she could travel back in time, Sharon tells me there are two things she would have done differently: "First, I would have picked one of the areas I do business in to focus on. Second, I would have maintained a regular blog [see Figure 17-3]. With the explosive growth of social media, I really believe that both of these items are musts for anyone as far as helping with personal branding goes. The situation I put myself in is that I'm known as being a jack of many trades (which I am), but it has probably meant less business this way."

When working with clients, Sharon stresses the importance of having a blog in place *before* you start work on developing a Twitter presence. She's just launched a site at BloggingToday.com to help small businesses set up their own blog — another insightful move on her part.

Sharon has also found that, due to the huge number of followers she now has, that time management has become more of an issue. "During my first year on Twitter, there were many days where I spent several hours

FIGURE 17-3

Sharon regrets not having started her blog sooner.

a day on the service. I was able to engage far more than I do now, but once I got to around 30,000 followers, it became too difficult to interact with people on a mass-conversational level. I used to love throwing out a question to everyone, see the responses come in, and have lengthy discussions as a result. Then it got to the point where the volume of responses was just too overwhelming.

"Currently, I spend 15 to 45 minutes a day most days on Twitter. This is typically split into a handful of short visits. I'll share a song and for the duration of the song, I'll respond to some of the incoming tweets I've received, retweet one or more things I see from others, and share a couple of things myself. About two-thirds of my tweets are engaging with others. However, most of the tweets interacting with others publicly are lighter in nature. I'll quickly route serious or extended discussions off Twitter.

"When I come across interesting content during my day, I'll save it for sharing on Twitter. I don't go out of my way to find things to share and I try to limit self-promotional tweets to maybe one in 50 or 100 tweets."

Sharon Hayes' Golden Rules for Personal Branding on Twitter

Here are Sharon's ten personal tips for Twitter success:

1. Follow back

Although it looks nice to have more followers than you are following, if you are serious about building a personal brand, I believe adopting 'follow all back' (at least for real people) is a good strategy. As I've suggested, a lot of business can be generated by referrals."

2. Use keywords in your bio

Make sure your bio reads well and uses keywords pertinent to what you do, and ensure everything is spelled correctly. Appropriate keywords can help people find you. The rest is about making sure you project a professional image."

3. Save the best till last

"If you tweet in spurts like I do, try to make sure that your last few tweets are representative of you and what you share on Twitter. For example, make sure that if you interact with others, at least one @ reply shows in your last few tweets. Your last tweet should not be entirely self-promotional. This tip, along with the last one, will help improve the number of people who will follow you back."

4. Keep it human

"Many people recommend automating sending of tweets. One of the reasons given is to save time. Another reason is that with different time zones, it will allow you to reach more people. I don't advocate automatic tweeting. I've had clients who did this and had major glitches with links proving to be incorrect and other such disasters. At the same time, your followers may not realize you aren't actually there and it can be frustrating to see tweets coming from someone you've asked a question of, or commented to, and not received a response on. Keep the human component in your tweets!"

5. Don't ruffle any feathers!

"Be neutral on hot topics outside of your core competency. Unless you are a fantastic debater, it's not worth ruffling feathers and getting into heated discussions with followers."

6. Remember quality takes time

"At a certain point, it's best to let your following base grow organically. If you are consistent with your message and doing things right on Twitter, you'll continue to get new followers. These will be people who are actually interested in the content you share. The number of followers you have on Twitter doesn't matter, it's the quality. It takes time to build relationships with people."

7. Don't tweet in a bad mood

"If you're having a bad day, you may want to rethink whether you should go on Twitter. The world won't fall apart if you don't tweet one day, but you could do damage to your reputation and personal brand if you interact with others when you aren't in good form."

8. Keep it upbeat!

"Keep your complaints to a minimum. Many people go on Twitter as a means to escape. They don't want to be subjected to unnecessary negativity. Unless, of course, being a downer is your thing! So, try and keep it upbeat."

9. Inject your tweets with brand 'you'

"You want to inject some of your own personality into things. If you share links, try and add your own comments to them. Don't be a broadcast-only channel; instead, interact and engage with others.

Also keep in mind that most people recognize avatars more than names. When building a personal brand, you should always use a photograph of yourself. I believe it's important to make sure that if you change photos, it should still be apparent that it is you. I've had some disasters when changing my photo where many people didn't recognize me. As a result my retweet volume and engagement level dropped dramatically."

10. Reciprocity rules

"Remember that reciprocity rules in social media! On Twitter, this means that if you want others to share your content, share theirs. Don't ask people to retweet something of yours if you've never interacted with them or shared something of theirs. I'd actually suggest not asking in general. Avoid using the Twitter retweet button; instead manually retweet because this gets more visibility."

Sharon Hayes' Favorite Twitter Tools

Sharon uses three primary Twitter tools: CoTweet, Friendorfollow. com, and Twitter Lists.

CoTweet is a web-based Twitter management platform that allows you to see your mentions, your stream, individual profiles of people, and previous exchanges with users, as well as have saved searches running. The platform also provides built-in reporting of who is retweeting your content and when, what your top content retweeted is, and more. Sharon had used other third-party applications to view statistics, but found the ones provided in CoTweet to be the most robust and the most accurate because they also show protected users.

CoTweet lets you schedule tweets and, although she doesn't send out tweets when she's not around, Sharon will schedule some tweets to go out at intervals, so that they don't flood less active users' streams. "In five or ten minutes, I can easily reply to ten or 20 tweets, but I will queue them to go out over a half hour or hour."

Sharon also loves the history feature of CoTweet, where she can view all past communications with a specific user. "It saves me from having to remember details," she says.

Sharon also uses Friendorfollow.com's paid version because it allows her to "unfollow those who have unfollowed me. It is the only tool I've found to be accurate in showing who is or isn't following," she claims.

Additionally, Sharon is an extensive user of Twitter Lists (shown in Figure 17-4). She has broken her lists into multiple ones, including those for people who retweet her, news sources, and closest friends. Twitter Lists has saved her a considerable amount of time finding those things she wants to reshare or respond to.

Sharon believes that the Twitter tools she uses have enabled her to spend less time on the platform, without being any less effective in her

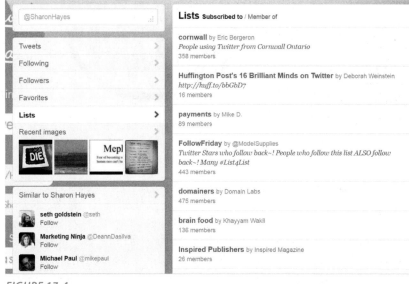

FIGURE 17-4

Sharon has found Twitter Lists to be a great way to organize her followers.

stream. "All told, with the way I manage my Twitter account and the tools I use, it is rare that I spend more than three hours a week on Twitter. This is without any kind of automation!"

Sharon shows that you don't need to have a permanent Twitter presence to make a powerful impact. What you do need is a strong personal brand message that translates well in the tweets you do choose to send out each day, and that's something that Sharon has in buckets!

"Every day of my life is now magic because of Twitter.
I am discovering amazing people and feel increasingly
empowered."

@mqtodd

18

The 'Green' Giant of Twitter

Michael Q. Todd (@mqtodd) is one of those rare individuals who has taken to social media like a duck to water. He juggles all his platforms (actually, he admits to being a juggling addict!) with what appears to be the greatest of ease and yet he readily engages and provides value to his ever-growing flock of Twitter followers.

Michael's a true giant in leadership and expertise, and this chapter tells his inspirational personal branding story through his own experiences of using Twitter.

In Search of a Meaningful Life

Michael has worked as a lawyer in various locations around the world, but he always felt that something was missing.

"I woke up a couple of years ago and realized that I was born to do something meaningful with my life. I first found Facebook then Twitter as places where you can find like-minded and passionate people who are also determined to make a difference.

"I joined Twitter in late February 2009 but never really knew what it was about until May of that year, when I started delving deeper into the whole nature of the platform and sought out some mentors. I never considered giving up on it, as I could see it growing. I just couldn't crack the code at the time and felt that I wasn't making progress. Then I got involved with a movement called #IranRevolution. I tweeted like crazy, turned my hair green in sympathy [green is a color associated with the revolution] with the oppressed tweeters in Iran [see Figure 18-1], and have never looked back."

FIGURE 18-1

Michael's Twitter profile gives an insight into the man behind the tweets.

Hang in There!

Michael finds it sad that 97 to 98 percent of people give up on Twitter in the first few months. "It's a different kind of place compared to any other social networking or marketing platform and, because of this, some unlearning of traditional marketing and communicating practices needs to be done. Unlearning is often much harder than learning!

"One of the real beauties of Twitter is that everyone can and does have their own way of doing things. There is no right or wrong way! Heaven help that everyone copies my way of doing things exactly.

"During June 2009 in Tokyo, I was lucky enough to hear Evan Williams, one of the founders of Twitter, explain what a platform is. He said, 'It's a place for an open exchange of ideas and information.'"

A Constantly Evolving Platform

Michael often compares the early days of Twitter with the early days of the Internet. "Twitter is being built like the Internet was built. The Internet started around 1990 as a very basic platform for an individual to have a presence through a single-page website. Soon, companies got involved too and one page for each website grew to become two and more.

"Twitter is continually adding features itself but, even more excitingly, it welcomes others to develop features by way of applications that make Twitter a more interesting and useful place to spend time on, and so it is a constantly developing space.

"It has been amazing watching the rapid take-up of Twitter in Japan in the past few months. I have heard that use has tripled in the past year in Japan, and the country is now responsible for 12 percent of tweets worldwide, making it rank third in the countries with the most Twitter accounts [see Figure 18-2].

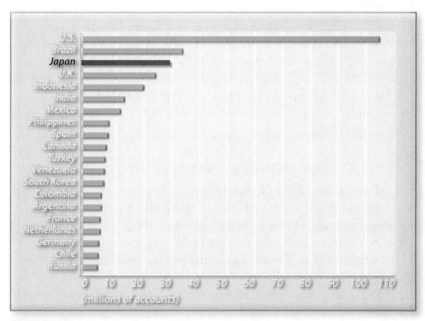

FIGURE 18-2

A 2012 study by Semiocast found that Japan's use of Twitter has risen exponentially in 2011, ranking at Number 3 globally as of January 1, 2012.

"It is clear that Twitter is set for massive worldwide expansion, as more and more 'get' what it is about and experience the power and fun of using it."

Michael Todd's Golden Rules for Personal Branding Success

Michael has ten best practices for successful personal branding.

1. The name has it!

"Your Twitter username can be anything up to 15 characters but, as you will find, most of the good ones are gone. The best way to search for names is to go to Twitter itself and then play around with names from there. You can use underscore or numbers as well as the letters of the alphabet when making your Twitter name but I recommend using your own name with no underscores or numbers.

"Also avoid doing such things as using a 5 instead of an S. Make it as easy as possible for people to remember your name. The shorter the better is also good. If you have a shorter name it makes it easier for people to fit your name into tweets. I had a difficult time balancing this, as @michaelqtodd was very long and many people found it difficult to spell Michael. So I changed my Twitter handle to @mqtodd. As a result, I found myself being added to more lists as well as having more people conversing with me."

2. That all-important bio

"As well as your name, your location is also important in your bio, as many people search for and add people to lists based on this information. Recently, I have divided my time between Tokyo, Japan, and Brisbane, Australia, so for location I have put Tokyo and Brisbane. If you live in, say, Shanghai, it may be good to put 'Shanghai, China' as it may attract more searches.

"Then you have the chance to nominate a website and most people use their blog, business website, or link to their Facebook page. Next, you'll need to write about yourself in 160 characters. Check out what others in your niche are saying about themselves, but if you can be funny and authentic, that is best. Remember to use searchable keywords in your bio."

3. Say cheese!

"Next is an important thing: your photo. Show your face and present yourself as a friendly and approachable member of the social community. It's as simple as that. People like people like themselves. You have only a second or so to attract them, so smile and work your charm on the camera lens. If you can make your photo more memorable, that is a plus. Some of us even adorn ourselves with hats or even Photoshopped wigs."

4. Keep it public wherever possible

"In its most basic form, Twitter is a way to send out short messages, both privately (like an text message) and more especially publicly. It is also a search engine for those public messages. Some people also choose to protect their tweets so they can be seen only by friends, but if you want to brand yourself, please do not do this.

"The next time you send an e-mail, a text message, or a Facebook update, think about sending it out as a tweet instead."

5. Retweets are your Twitter gems

"Retweeting is a vital and often underused part of Twitter, and research shows that only about 3 percent of tweets are retweets. I suggest that to get Twitter really humming when you start that at least 30 to 40 percent of your tweets are retweets.

"If your tweet is not merely conversation and you want it shared to the world as much as possible, you should keep it to 115 to 120 characters so that it can be retweeted once or twice — or maybe even three times. Make it easy for people to retweet you and even make a comment.

"It's this ability for tweets and links to be shared outside your own followers or circle of influence that contributes to making Twitter so magical."

6. Review how others perceive you

"By looking at your last 20 tweets, you should be able to easily see what three things your account is mainly about. You will also quickly see how others perceive you by the subjects of the lists that have added you. Pay lots of attention to this and adjust accordingly.

"Tweet five to eight times a day about things in your niche. Make about half of these retweets. If you can, make a short relevant comment when you retweet. Make another 20 to 30 percent of your tweets about blog posts or articles that you have found and liked.

"To shorten your links, get an account at Bit.ly or use a Twitter client such as HootSuite or TweetDeck to shorten them for you.

"Another 5 percent of so of your tweets can be about you, and another 20 percent or so can be made up of conversations just as you would when sending a text message."

7. Find the right people to follow

"To find the key people to follow and to retweet, I recommend using Twitter directories such as Twellow and TweetFind. You can also find people by using the Find People function in the Twitter search function. You can search for people both by their Twitter name and their real-life name.

"Follow the people who you find are talking to and retweeting your key people — those who are most influential in your particular areas of interest. If you are visibly intelligent and communicative in your particular niche, these people will also naturally be interested in you and will check you out and probably follow you back."

8. Take part in Follow Fridays (#FF)

"I also recommend doing a Follow Friday (#FF) each week of the 10 to 15 key people you are interested in. This is a way of acknowledging that you like and recommend them. Also, it's useful to follow in terms of finding out who others are recommending. Use tools like FollowFriday Helper [shown in Figure 18-3] to find out who else has been tweeting about you and worth an #FF mention each week."

**follow @ffhelper
on Twitter**

What's #FF Helper about?

Simple. Most of the people I know do not recommend me because it's just too much work to do on the last day of the week. FollowFriday Helper is the solution to that.

But that's not all. You can use FFH on other days - other than Fridays - to send #ThankYou, #Gratitude, #Top and about any other social tweet you might think of.

FIGURE 18-3

FollowFriday Helper is a great tool for finding out who's been mentioning you on Twitter each week.

9. Tweet regularly

"Like a lot of things in life, being regular, giving value, and being fun will attract people to you. Tweeting 40 minutes a day every day is much better than, say, 10 hours all on a Sunday."

10. Visualize your success

"Make your own style, and do not give up. Focus on staying true to your personal brand and visualize where you want it to take you. Huge success awaits!"

Michael Todd's Favorite Twitter Tools

Michael uses multiple tools to help him tweet. Here are a few that he especially recommends.

Chirpaloo

Chirpaloo enables you to manage your followers in a searchable database where their profile, tweets, website, social graph, and demographic data are instantly accessible. Users can now identify and categorize influencers, analyze, and engage in relevant conversations with groups and individuals in a way that has never been possible.

FIGURE 18-4

Twylah provides a magazine-style layout of Michael's most recent and popular tweets.

Twylah

Twylah (see Figure 18-4) allows users to create a website full of their recent and most popular tweets. Set out in topics of their choice pictorially. Users can also create power Tweets that get their own web page and can be commented on.

Ifttt

This great Twitter tool creates recipes of sharing actions to and from Twitter and several other social platforms. It also has an outstanding Twitter list-creation feature.

HashTracking

This tool shows how many times a hashtag has been used in the last 24 hours and provides an archive of every tweet with that hashtag. It also shows the ten most-followed people who have used the hashtag, along with a list of who has tweeted the hashtag the most.

Michael's personal branding success story is testimony to the value he provides to others on the platform on a daily basis. His popularity continues to grow, and rightly so.

"Relationships and engagement are today's new currency"

#TeamGratton

19

Twitter to the Power of Two

There's something about Twitter that brings people together, and it's not just on a personal branding level. I can personally vouch that it has also enriched my marriage.

Starting out on Twitter as @grattongirl was very much an experiment for me in social networking, one that I never anticipated would take me so far in such a short space of time. Within months of joining, I was well and truly hooked and found myself talking incessantly about the platform to my husband Dean who, at the time, wasn't really into "the social networking thing," as he called it back then.

But I guess my enthusiasm paid off. Eventually Dean decided to take a closer look at the platform I couldn't get enough of. He initially signed up as @Dean_Gratton and promptly announced, "I don't get it!"

"Just hang in there," I told him with firm assurance, knowing that he was about to throw in the Twitter towel. He shrugged his shoulders in begrudging affirmation and asked me in an ambivalent tone, "So what do I do now?"

I explained to him what I had discovered myself: That Twitter wasn't all about idle breakfast food chitchat, but was a powerful search tool and a great identifier of news and connections in my respective arenas. "Try out the search feature," I prompted. "Use the words 'Bluetooth,' 'wireless,' or any other technology you're planning to feature in your new book."

A rise of his eyebrows told me he was a little more intrigued as he located the search feature on Twitter and began entering those all-important keywords. Several hours later he was still taking stock of everything he had managed to find and had to admit that Twitter had "blown him away."

"I had no idea so many people I need to contact are on Twitter," he remarked incredulously at dinner. "And the article links, the research papers — wow!"

And that was that! In a matter of hours, Dean was as hooked on Twitter as I. We chatted about its potential that night with all the excitement of a couple of children on Christmas Eve.

Going All the Way

And it got even better once Dean began tweeting himself. Like any virgin tweeter, he was slightly nervous to begin with, fumbling with his keyboard and rewording everything several times before clicking the Send button. But once he got the hang of it, there was no stopping him.

Again, Dean was blown away by the level of engagement he received. Always the geeky loner at school (Dean's nickname was The Professor), he was suddenly Mr. Popular on Twitter — and what's more, he loved it!

As the weeks went on, he began to show more and more of his personality through his tweets and to add humor and variety to the content

A Change of Handle

Then one day I received a tweet from a male admirer asking me, "Is there a @grattonboy in your life?" I laughed with Dean about it. "I'm your @grattonboy," he exclaimed, and then he jumped up as though struck by lightning. "That's it!" he yelled. "What?" I replied, slightly concerned by his outburst. "Don't you see?" he said, taking my hand. "@grattonboy! That should be my Twitter handle."

We talked about it some more and decided that it was still relatively early days for Dean on Twitter, so changing his handle shouldn't be too much of a problem. We also acknowledged that @grattonboy was the obvious choice of name, considering my more-established Twitter persona as @grattongirl.

The next day, Dean informed his followers of his decision to change his handle to @grattonboy and his reason behind it. Suddenly the two of us were well and truly a Twitter couple and our united personal branding had begun (see Figure 19-1).

Twitter's Cutest Couple

Being a Twitter couple has been a rewarding personal branding exercise and very much a fun learning curve. To begin with, Dean and I would sneak in tweets referring to each other affectionately and sometimes recalling amusing stories about our life together. Over time, we became known as the cutest couple on Twitter (see Figure 19-2) and

Sarah-Jayne Gratton
@grattongirl
Celebrity author, host & Twitter brandologist. In the 'Sunday Times Social List' & in 'Twitter's Top 75 Badass Women' #BA75 (wife of @grattonboy) #TeamGratton
London, United Kingdom   http://www.sarahjaynegratton.com

Edit your profile

71,063 TWEETS
29,679 FOLLOWING
110,603 FOLLOWERS

Dean Anthony Gratton
@grattonboy   FOLLOWS YOU
Dean (hubby to @grattongirl) is a superb cook, foodie, wine lover, bestselling author & columnist. He's a social media persona & Twitter 'Top Dog' #TeamGratton
London, United Kingdom   http://www.deangratton.com

Following

86,365 TWEETS
27,009 FOLLOWING
114,905 FOLLOWERS

FIGURE 19-1

Dean's changing his Twitter handle to @grattonboy fully united our personal brands.

increasingly began to receive tweets addressing the two of us jointly, as well as individually.

As the number of our followers began increasing, we began to learn the tips and tricks of using Twitter in a way that allowed us to maximize our personal brand success on the platform. We were truly beginning to spread our Twitter wings and we weren't afraid to try new things, including many of the Twitter tools that were being developed and that I cover in Part Four.

After several years on Twitter, I began to offer professional advice to new Twitter users and to help them create and promote their personal brand message. I was still very much involved in writing for the theater, and several of my screenplays had been optioned by major studios, but my fascination with using Twitter for personal branding became something of an obsession that led me to focus more and more on writing articles on the subject.

In 2010, our personal branding success on Twitter brought about an amazing opportunity. Dean and I were offered a contract to write a book about how to succeed in social media. The book was to be called *Zero to*

Lori McNee
@lorimcneeartist

Following

Waving hello to Twitter's cutest couple! >
@grattonboy & @grattongirl

↩ Reply   ⇄ Retweet   ★ Favorite   ≋ Buffer

FIGURE 19-2

Our union on Twitter earned us the title "cutest couple."

100,000. We used Twitter to publicize our progress, of course, and to discuss our intended chapters (along with venting our incessant need for caffeine) to our rapidly growing band of loyal followers.

As time progressed and the book grew near to completion, we tweeted promotional quotes using the hashtags #Zeroto100000 and #TeamGratton, along with links to the pre-order sites and the book's own website.

Once launched, we invited readers to tweet their personal reviews of the book (see Figure 19-3), which they did in the thousands. It was a heady time for us both and one that proved to be a great marketing campaign for the book.

From that point on, the hashtag #TeamGratton stuck and was soon being used outside the book's promotional tweets. The hashtag identified us as both a couple and a brand that was becoming increasingly popular and powerful in the Twitter community.

One day, a promotions company asked us to review and endorse their products on Twitter. This began a steady stream of similar offers, some with a pay-check attached and all with the opportunity to receive a wide variety of products that were linked to the #TeamGratton group of interests. Together, we tested everything — wireless headphones, wine, and household appliances.

FIGURE 19-3

Using the hashtag #TeamGratton, we asked readers of our book to tweet their reviews.

We must have done something right because the companies involved continue to use us to promote anything new they develop. This experience really drove home to us the effectiveness of using a loyal personal brand as a tool for recommendation and market progression.

These days, people buy into brand personality rather than a staid product description. It's a powerful lesson, one that I relay to my clients again and again.

#TeamGratton's Golden Rules for Personal Branding Success

This list touches on many of the things I covered in Part Two of this book, as well as provides a few extra nuggets of information that will help you build your own personal branding success story.

1. Learn how to listen

The first step to personal branding success on Twitter is to listen to the conversation before getting involved. Think of starting out as going on a blind date.

You want to find out as much as you can about your partner before divulging too much about yourself, so take time to find out about those tweets and tweeters that are of interest and value to you through using Twitter's #Discover pane options such as Stories, Find Friends, and Browse Categories (see Figure 19-4); it provides a range of topical content tailored to your bio.

2. Spot and optimize trends in your brand sector

Look for those trends and themes that come up again and again in your sectors of interest. Use them to provide topics of discussion and value to your followers. Find new angles on articles you have read, comment on blog posts, and tweet about them. Share the topics that get you noticed as your enthusiasm will encourage others to join in the conversation.

3. Harmonize your personal brand voice

Think of your personal brand message as your social voice; a harmony of those facets of your personality that best reflect your brand

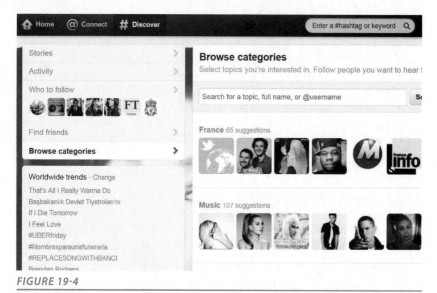

FIGURE 19-4

Find and listen to what others are tweeting about using Twitter's #Discover feature.

message. Remember that your brand and your social voice are one and the same. Traditional media experts may have tried to separate them, but their dated philosophy fails to embrace the shift in communication that Twitter has been fundamental in bringing about.

It may take a little time to fine-tune your voice so, go easy on yourself and don't rush things. For Dean and me, it was a matter of building our personal brand confidence through Twitter engagement and response, where little by little, our personalities began to shine through our tweets.

4. Use cross-platform promotion

I introduce cross-platform promotion (CPP) in Chapter 8 and mention it throughout the book many times, particularly in the other personal branding success stories in Part Three.

Remember that CPP involves spreading your message across *all* your social media platforms using Twitter as your primary platform for exposure. Include links in your tweets to your blog posts, website, Facebook, and Google+ accounts, and invite people to connect with you there, too (see Figure 19-5).

Acknowledge comments given on your blog through your tweets, and tweet thanks to those people sharing your brand content. Encourage the

Sarah-Jayne Gratton
@grattongirl

Join me on Google+:goo.gl/eFqOe

← Reply 🗑 Delete ★ Favorite ⮩ Buffer

FIGURE 19-5

I use cross-platform promotion (CPP) to encourage my followers to connect with me on my other social networks.

flow of information through connecting your cross-platform promotion links in Twitter chats and discussions. Be creative, and don't forget to share other links of interest, too (see Figure 19-6).

5. Create a Twittertorial calendar

As Chapter 7 explains, a Twittertorial calendar is an idea derived from a publication's editorial calendar. It's a means of organizing the content you have curated in easily scheduled posts that can be taken and formulated in your personal brand show on Twitter.

You Twittertorial calendar should embrace the four types of tweet introduced in Chapter 5: share, inform, thank, and engage (SITE). Blending them will over time become second nature to you, but in the early days pay careful attention to how you mix them throughout the day to gauge the optimum blend for your personal brand.

6. Beware the narcissists and trolls

Social media narcissism is very real and can be a negative influence on your personal brand if left unchecked. As you become more involved

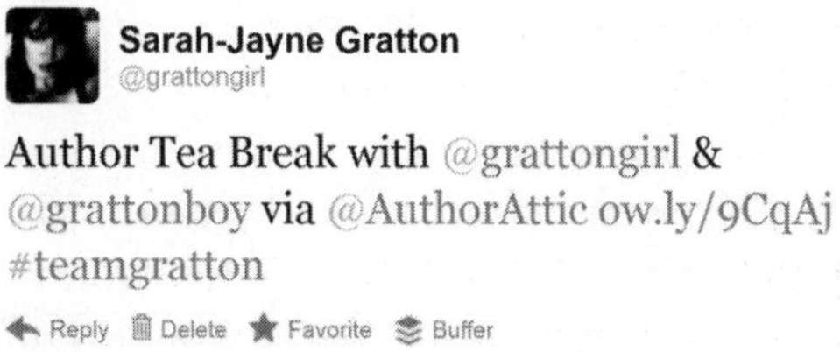

Sarah-Jayne Gratton
@grattongirl

Author Tea Break with @grattongirl & @grattonboy via @AuthorAttic ow.ly/9CqAj #teamgratton

← Reply 🗑 Delete ★ Favorite ⮩ Buffer

FIGURE 19-6

#TeamGratton creatively uses cross-platform promotion to promote interviews.

on Twitter, you'll almost certainly encounter it, along with those Internet trolls who like nothing more than the opportunity to criticize others online (and most likely offline, too).

It will probably happen to you too: that moment of complete ego-driven mania, fueled by having achieved a certain number of followers. One minute you may be tweeting about the importance of sharing and the next you're so seduced by all the responses and comments surrounding your wonderful Twitter show that you begin to feel like the new messiah! This is your red light, your signal to take a reality check and come back down to earth.

Social media narcissists are for the most part shallow and volatile. They take far more than they give out on their platforms, and it really isn't worth investing your time on them. Participating in the world of the trolls and narcissists will only cause you setbacks on your road to personal branding success.

7. Schedule for success

As you know by now, I'm an advocate of scheduling your tweets, provided it's done in the right way, using the right tools, and without losing that all important time for engagement with your followers. No matter how much you may want to avoid it, as your Twitter following grows, scheduling becomes more and more necessary to ensure that you have a global Twitter presence that works for your brand around the clock. Part Four takes you step by step with the best scheduling tools, enabling you to find the right ones for you.

8. Become a botinator

I introduce the concept of becoming a botinator in Chapter 6 and explain how in terms of quality and quantity of followers, it absolutely *is* possible to have it all!

Bots are definitely not quality followers, so keep your eyes open for them and remember the warning signs: A stream of junk or spam tweets indicates that these are most likely being sent from a bot. Also bear in mind that bots like to take different Twitter handles to repeatedly push the same content, so make a note of any tweets that look particularly suspicious and watch for recurrences.

Peruse the Twitter streams of any new followers to make sure they aren't just blanket posting with no real purpose or interest in others. Paying attention will provide an immediate impression of their value.

9. Use hashtags and start a trending topic

Follow my tried-and-tested formula for creating a trending topic that I detail in Chapter 10. Study the topics that are currently trending and look for patterns that can link them to your hashtag. But don't place unrelated hashtags in other trending topic tweets because doing so can get you in your follower's bad graces. Instead, seek out content and links pertaining to what's being tweeted about and use your hashtags to reinforce the message.

10. Have fun!

All our personal branding success stories have one constant underlying element: They are all based on enjoying Twitter and having fun while tweeting. Twitter should never be a chore. If it is, reassess how you're using it and what's hindering your enjoyment.

#TeamGratton's Favorite Twitter Tools

Normally, I'd write about the Twitter tools that have made a difference to my personal brand and contributed to it becoming a success. But instead of adding just a few personal paragraphs, I've decided to feature a whole section of the book on the subject: Part Four.

There are so many wonderful tools out there, and choosing the right ones will dramatically enhance your personal branding endeavors, saving you time and making your Twitter experience a far more pleasurable one.

So, turn the page and start exploring all the options in Part Four. You'll find it an immensely valuable guide that will enable you to create your own Twitter toolkit.

Part Four

Twitter Toolkit: Supercharge Your Brand

Every Twitter toolkit is personal.
Each tool in it makes building and
maintaining your personal brand an
easier and more enjoyable journey of
continual discovery.

Your Twitter Toolbox

In this final part, you can explore at your leisure and dip into whenever you need a helping hand from one of the many Twitter tools and services I feature. All have been chosen with simplicity and usefulness in mind. Most are free, a fact that doesn't deter from their value in helping you to manage your daily use of Twitter and to supercharge your online brand message.

I call it your Twitter toolbox because that's exactly what it is! Whether it's help in curating the right content, scheduling your tweets, or tracking your success versus your competitors, you can delve into your toolbox whenever you feel the need to arm yourself with a new resource.

You'll find some of the tools particularly relevant when you're starting out on Twitter, whereas others fit better further down the line of experience. Above all, I hope the tools I've included encourage you to do your own homework and discover new ones of your own.

"To seek new friends and stranger companies."

—A Midsummer Night's Dream

20

Twitter Clients and Directories

Twitter clients provide an interface for tweeting and organizing your followers, favorite tweets, Twitter lists, and other points of interest that help make building your personal brand on Twitter an enjoyable and manageable experience. However, finding the right Twitter client can prove to be a daunting task, given the sheer number of clients available.

Choosing Your Perfect Twitter Client

The Twitter client market is *massive*. There are literally hundreds of clients available, spanning every desktop and mobile platform. I've selected the ones that offer both advanced features and ease of use to maximize your Twitter experience. My advice is to try a few and see which ones best fit your personal branding needs. All these products are free, with the exception of HootSuite, which has a $9.99-per-month pro version.

Twitter

When you compare the native Twitter design to other Twitter clients (see Figure 20-1), the first thing you'll notice is that the layout is much more like a traditional blog.

On the right, your stream of tweets is listed; clicking one brings up details on the tweet and any supported media file attached to the tweet.

On the left, you get access to key statistics about your account, including tweet and follower count, as well as the current trending topics and a quick composition window for new tweets.

Another notable point is that Twitter is branded to match your profile, so the site's background image reflects the one you chose or uploaded for your profile.

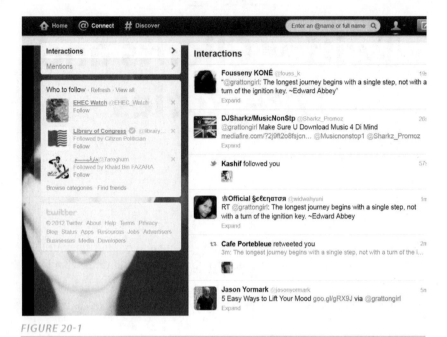

FIGURE 20-1

The native Twitter client is in a continual state of evolution.

It's a formula that works for many, but some users find it clumsy and rather basic for their personal branding needs. Twitter is, however, in a continual state of evolution with new features rolled out on a regular basis so don't rule it out as your Twitter client of choice.

HootSuite

HootSuite (see Figure 20-2) is both a web- and a mobile-based Twitter client (free for the basic version and $9.99 per month for the pro version, which enhances its multiuser and analytics capabilities) designed to manage multiple social media platforms, including Facebook, LinkedIn, and Google+. It can handle multiple Twitter accounts and produce reports based on custom analytics to track your brand awareness, follower growth, and other pertinent demographic data.

HootSuite is the Twitter client I use on my desktop every day. I love the fact that it lets me click through follower statistics and create reports for my clients. It can work with multiple profiles and schedule tweets from its dashboard. Being browser-based, HootSuite also lets you log in

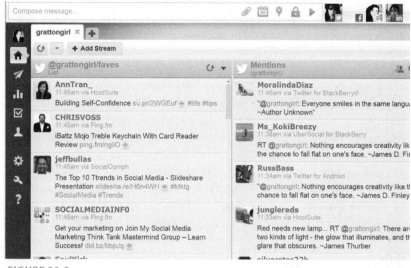

FIGURE 20-2

HootSuite offers advanced features including report creation and team collaboration.

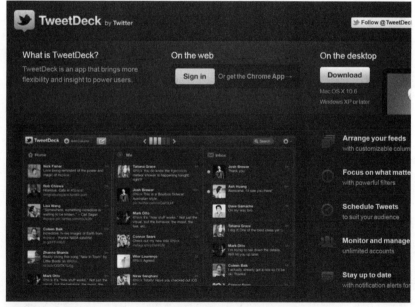

FIGURE 20-3

TweetDeck is a free Twitter client with a wealth of advanced features.

from any computer. You can also download the HootSuite app for iPhone, iPad, and Android mobile devices for tweeting on the go.

TweetDeck

TweetDeck (see Figure 20-3), acquired by Twitter in 2011, is a social media dashboard application for managing Twitter and other social network accounts. It was undoubtedly the leading client outside of Twitter before the emergence of HootSuite, and it is still a popular choice due to its advanced features such as multiaccount management, scheduling, filtering, and column customization.

Once only available as an Adobe AIR application, it now has versions for several operating systems, including Windows, OS X, Chrome OS, Linux, iOS (for the iPad and iPhone), and Android.

FIGURE 20-4

Janetter is one of the most flexible and customizable Twitter clients and claims to be "the best on the Net!"

Janetter

Janetter (see Figure 20-4) claims to be "the best Twitter client on the net" and, although that claim is open to debate, there's no doubt that Janetter has a lot of flexibility. There's a multicolumn view, support for multiple accounts, 27 themes, customizable fonts and display formats, wallpaper, notifications, auto-complete, keyboard shortcuts, and language translation. If you're using the Windows version, you can even create your own themes using HTML.

DestroyTwitter

An unusual name for such a useful and featured-packed Twitter client! DestroyTwitter (see Figure 20-5) is a powerful Adobe AIR app with an interface that's as big or as small as you want. Available for Windows,

FIGURE 20-5

A powerful yet memory-light Twitter client, DestroyTwitter is growing in popularity.

OS X, and Linux, it lets you go full-screen with customizable, multiple columns, or you can simply tuck it away in a corner of your desktop.

DestroyTwitter boasts an excellent range of filters, an array of customization options, username auto-completion, appealing notifications, and a small memory footprint, although it doesn't support multiple Twitter accounts.

Seesmic

Seesmic (see Figure 20-6) has become one of the most popular social software clients, and rightly so. It lets you easily access all your social networks from its dashboard and has an abundance of advanced features such as customizable columns, advanced search, scheduling, geo-tagging, and translation ability. It's available via the web or as a standalone desktop or mobile application.

Designed to easily manage and build your community directly in your browser, it processes your messages in an e-mail-like interface and lets you comprehensively view and manage your Twitter lists.

FIGURE 20-6

Seesmic is an advanced social client that manages to cram in a wealth of features in an easy to use dashboard format.

Twitter Directories

Twitter directories are places to search and find new Twitter users to follow based on your interests. The directories are great starting points for finding the influencers in your sector. I've listed my favorites here and suggest that you register with them all for maximum personal brand exposure.

Twellow

Twellow (see Figure 20-7) is *the* Twitter version of the Yellow Pages. It was one of the first Twitter directories and anyone who is anybody is listed in it.

Use Twellow to browse through Twitter users to find those worth following or list yourself to promote your personal brand and build your following.

FIGURE 20-7

Twellow is widely known as the Twitter Yellow Pages and is a must-use Twitter directory.

FIGURE 20-8

Listorious locates the influential people you need to add to your following based on name, keyword, or tag.

Just Tweet It

Another widely used directory, Just Tweet It is a useful starting point to locate those influential tweeters you need to follow.

Listorious

Listorious (see Figure 20-8) is another free must-have tool for your Twitter toolkit. It is a people directory, but it's also a directory of Twitter lists. It lets you search thousands of lists, sorted in several different ways, including by topic tag.

Connect.Me

When I was invited to join Connect.Me (see Figure 20-9), I quickly saw the benefits of doing so. When you sign up, you create what Connect. Me terms "your social business card." By creating your card, you are effectively turning your social networks into your personal reputation network.

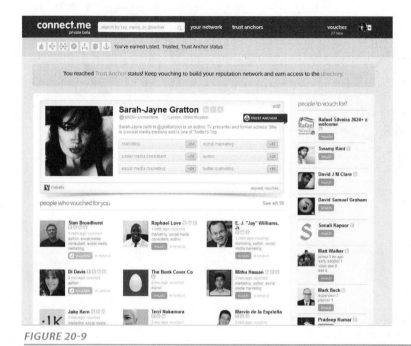

FIGURE 20-9

Connect.Me is a new way of locating the influencers you need to follow and of building your own online influence through a vouching system.

You can also control your online identity and reputation, and — unlike other tools — Connect.Me uses peer-to-peer vouching to build your reputation instead of algorithms to calculate influence.

"There are more things in heaven and earth, Horatio."

—*Hamlet*

21

Curation Tools

Finding great content is key to building your personal brand and to keep it soaring in the social stratosphere on Twitter and your other social platforms. Finding a continual flow of exciting and informative content for your personal brand show can, however, be a time-consuming and stressful activity if not approached in the right way.

This chapter to showcases what I believe are the best tools for the job. Those that will make your curation a breeze and ensure that your content is always fresh, relevant, informative, and entertaining. Even better is that, with the exception of Intigi, they are free to use.

Blog Alternatives

A great website or blog that updates its readers with a new flow of information is something that every personal brand needs, but there are some of us who shy away from the prospect of writing a new blog post every couple of days. Some struggle with writing, while others simply can't find the time to research and write new material on a continual basis. Either way, there are several great tools available that take the hard work out of putting together a great online publication that readers can subscribe to and that you can use to promote your personal brand through, using cross-platform promotion (CPP) with Twitter

Storify

Storify (shown in Figure 21-1) is a free tool that lets you curate content to tell stories using social media such as tweets, photos, and videos. It lets you search multiple social networks from one place and then drag individual elements into

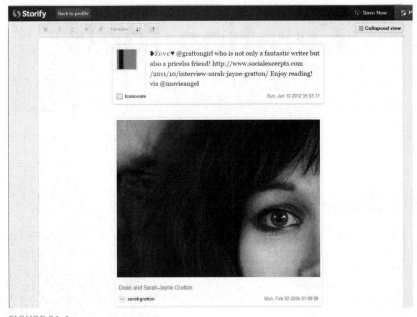

FIGURE 21-1

Storify lets you easily source content from around the web and lay it out in story form to share with your followers.

your story. You can then reorder the elements and also add text to give context to your readers. Storify is a very useful content-curation tool that also crosses the border into the realm of blogging and online publication, where you are, in effect, creating your own personal-brand magazine.

Scoop.it

Scoop.it (see Figure 21-2) is a new form of publishing-by-curation platform. Use the dashboard to manage multiple sources, including websites, RSS feeds, and social media accounts, and plug in relevant keywords and date parameters for more refined searching. Scoop.it is another free tool that provides a blog-alternative, letting you produce a customized content magazine for your followers.

FIGURE 21-2

Scoop.it lets you create a personal-brand magazine and is a great and easy alternative to setting up a blog.

Paper.li

Paper.li (see Figure 21-3) is my newspaper creator of choice. I use it to produce my web daily "newspaper," The @grattongirl Review, which since its launch has quickly grown in subscribers, with articles retweeted more than 100,000 times. Essentially, Paper.li is a free content-curation service that lets you publish your own personally named newspaper based on your personal-brand topics of interest. It lets your followers subscribe to it and delivers a fresh edition to them every day via an e-mail or tweet.

Twylah

Twylah (see Figure 21-4) is a free, auto-generated tool that bases your magazine on what's currently trending in your Twitter stream. It relies on tweets sent by or featuring you, so it's best used when your Twitter account is up and running and when you have established a good stream

FIGURE 21-3

Paper.li is a great newspaper-creation blog alternative tool for your personal brand.

FIGURE 21-4

Twylah auto-generates a magazine that showcases your trending tweets of content. It's easy to use because it does all the work for you, picking the tweets that others are talking about and sharing.

Twylah also lets you send what it calls a *power tweet*, where your tweet leads others to its own page on Twylah, so it acts as a showcase for your Twylah publication, encouraging people to enjoy and share more of your content.

Content Search Tools

I like to think of the following curation tools as intelligent search engines that let you quickly find and tailor content for your Twittertorial calendar. They all vary in features and ease of use, but all are highly effective in what they do.

YourVersion

Unlike traditional search engines, the free YourVersion (see Figure 21-5) is optimized to provide real-time updates tailored to your specific interests on a continuous basis. The YourVersion team likes to call it a "discovery engine."

YourVersion pulls together the most recent online gems related to your interests without requiring all that searching. Adding an interest like "iPhone" in YourVersion brings you not only the latest news on apps, but also includes blog posts, web pages, tweets, and videos. And you don't have to type "iPhone" in again; next time you visit YourVersion, the latest iPhone stories are waiting for you.

YourVersion lets you enter and save any interest in your profile. It's incredibly easy to use and lets you personalize your results in numerous ways. If you enter your keyword-based interests, YourVersion scours the web and blends discovered content into one easy-to-manage dashboard organized into tabs such as News, Blogs, Web, Twitter, Quora, and Friends. Use the Relevant versus Recent dial to get the right blend of content to share with your followers.

Intigi

Intigi was founded in 2011 by Jeff Ward, Joachim Hund, and Michael J. Fern, who were seeking to conduct content marketing for their software development and consulting businesses. Its goal is to reduce the friction

FIGURE 21-5

YourVersion provides real-time updates tailored to your specific interests.

in content marketing so that brands can focus their efforts on creating and curating valuable content for their followers.

With Intigi, you can set up interests using keywords. You can then monitor your favorite blogs and news sources, your Twitter accounts, and 30,000 online sources curated by Intigi users. It's then easy to organize your interests into folders. For example, you might create separate folders for content marketing, intelligence gathering (including industry trends and competitor information), and personal interests.

Search results can be filtered by different time windows, such as 24 hours or 7 days, and sorted by relevance or date. Sources can be limited to just your own or to all those available through Intigi.

Intigi's pricing starts at $9 per month for individuals, $19 for small businesses, and $49 for larger businesses and agencies; there's a 14-day free trial available.

Marginize

Marginize (see Figure 21-6) is a free browser plugin that augments every page on the web with a sidebar that lets users see what the world is

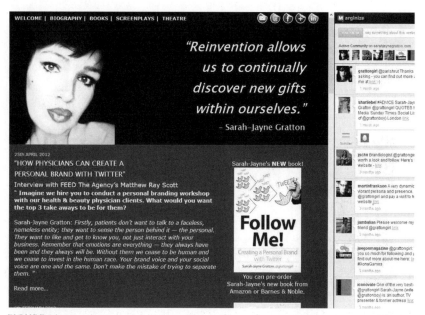

FIGURE 21-6

Marginize is the web browser equivalent of Foursquare and a fun way to share new content with your followers while mapping your virtual footprint.

saying about that page on Twitter and Facebook and interact with each other through comments and check-ins.

Not only is Marginize an innovative way to share content through Twitter, it's also a compelling way to create an online profile of where you have been. Think of it as a virtual version of Foursquare that lets you check in on websites or web pages that you go to. Each time you share an article, share a web page, or just have something that you want to say on a site, you are documenting your online footprint and, as with Foursquare, winning badges along the way.

Ultimately Marginize is a lot of fun and provides a way of sharing newly discovered web content with your followers.

StumbleUpon

StumbleUpon (see Figure 21-7) is an intelligent, free content browser that builds on your interests and preferences to locate great online content for you to share with your followers. You can save your favorites

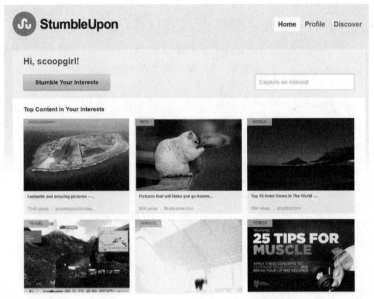

FIGURE 21-7

StumbleUpon is a long-standing favorite tool for content curation.

and tell it what you want to see less or more of by clicking the thumbs-down or thumbs-up buttons, respectively.

My only criticism of the tool is that some of the content located can be quite dated, so be sure to check the relevance before you include it in your Twittertorial calendar.

Tweet-Specific Tools

Sometimes, you want to assemble content from specific tweets. That's what these next two tools let you do.

Chirpstory

Chirpstory (see Figure 21-8) is a free, tweet-specific curation tool for telling and sharing stories from Twitter. You can organize favorite tweets, conversations, and themed hashtags together to create fun and easy-to-read narratives out of the Twitter experience. Simply drag tweets into a timeline, edit the results, and then share your "story" with the world.

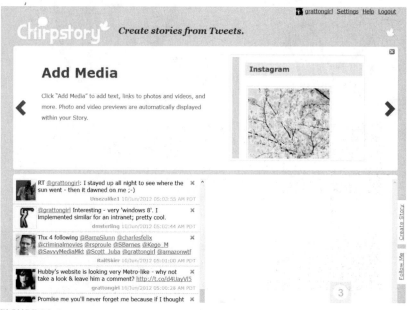

FIGURE 21-8

Chirpstory provides a tweet-focused curation experience.

Bag the Web

Bag the Web provides powerful, free web content capture in what it terms *bags*, which are assembled and linked to form collections of easily managed and sharable web content. The idea is simple and innovative — a bag can be filled with any topic and can also link to other relevant bags as references for particular content.

A bag takes just a few seconds to create. Just click the Create tab, add a title, and add a description; voilà, your bag is ready. If you want to keep a bag for personal use only, you can create it as private.

You can additionally copy and paste a web page's URL into the link adding box and keep it in any bag you create.

To make a bag even more powerful and useful you can add more links to other relevant bags. The tool also contains a very useful bookmarklet, which is a convenient tool you can add to your browser toolbar so you can add any web page you visit to any bag you create simply by clicking it.

"He cannot but with measure fit the honours
which we devise him."

—*Coriolanus*

22

Metrics and Analysis Tools

As you progress on Twitter, you'll want to see measurable exposure results for your personal brand, its reception in the Twitterverse, and look at aspects of your following to determine their value in the grand scheme of things. Twitter metrics can help you evaluate you social standing on Twitter and the effectiveness of your personal-brand show.

There are several tools to help you get this data, some free and others for a monthly or annual fee. All are well worth exploring and will provide you a wider view of how Twitter is benefitting brand "you."

Every Toolkit Needs a Good Measure

Understanding your social metrics means finding what I like to call your *elite social drivers*. These drivers are the most valuable traffic-driving sources across your social media platforms; in essence, your A-listers! The tools in this chapter provide everything you need to assess your performance, to establish what elements of your Twitter use need a little more oomph, and which ones deserve a round of applause.

Sprout Social

Tools such as Sprout Social track your social media activity and break it down through various analysis algorithms to provide all the necessary analytics to keep on top of your personal brand promotion.

This powerful tool emphasizes the four components of social media effectiveness: monitoring, engagement, measurement, and growth. Sprout Social gives you detailed information on followers, influence, engagement, and clicks, via intuitive charts and graphs. It lets you track the impact of your tweets, and you can even use it as your Twitter client by publishing and scheduling updates through it.

Social Sprout costs $39 per month for up to 20 social media profiles, $59 per month for up to 40 profiles, and $899 per month for unlimited profiles. There's a 30-day free trial available.

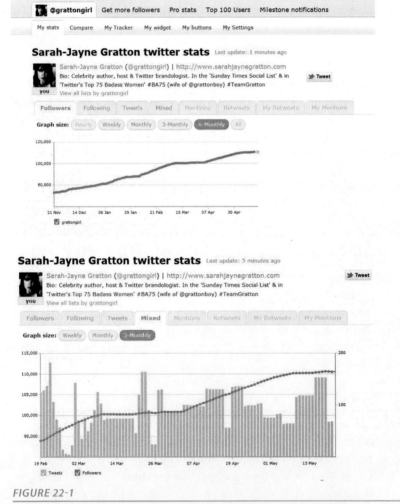

FIGURE 22-1

Twitter Counter is a great tool for showing your follower growth over time.

Twitter Counter

Twitter Counter (see Figure 22-1) is a useful tool to track your following. Simply type in the user name of the Twitter account you want to measure to have the results appear almost immediately in graph form. Ideally what you want to see in the graph is a steady pattern of growth, coupled with a continuous stream of mentions and retweets. There's a basic free service, but Twitter Counter also provide premium and pro-options, ranging from $15 to $150 per month, that let you export stats to Excel, compare users, download PDF reports, and create custom graphs.

Twitaholic

Twitaholic (see Figure 22-2) is a free tool that shows the growth of a Twitter account over time in terms of the number of new followers and follows. It also compares Twitter account followers by ranking them based on region. You simply type your Twitter handle in the search box and click the Go button to check your metrics. Twitaholic shows your rank in the Twittersphere based on several factors, including number of followers

FIGURE 22-2

Twitaholic ranks you according to number of followers and location.

and your geographic location. Your regional rank may be a helpful metric in identifying whether your account has the right amount of recognition for the geographic location it represents. For example, if you run a candy store in a small town in South Dakota, 300 followers may put you at the top of your region, showing that you have good recognition in your area.

Google Analytics

Google Analytics provides an effective, free method of tracking visitors from Twitter to other platforms such as your blog. To use it, you need to first install its code on your website or blog. The tool is compatible with many of the blogging sites, including WordPress and Blogger; both provide step-by-step details about how to incorporate Google Analytics on your site.

Once you have Google Analytics installed, you can extract visitor data by logging into the Google Analytics website and selecting your blog. Then click the Traffic Sources option (see Figure 22-3) in the top left corner. Next go to the Referring Sites pane and in the Find Sources box

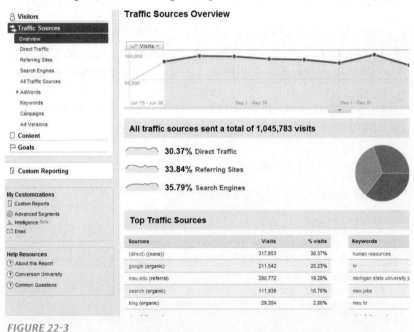

FIGURE 22-3

Google Analytics' Traffic Sources option lets you see how many visitors to your blog came from Twitter.

enter Twitter and click Go. A new chart and table appear, showing the number of visitors to your blog from Twitter.

Installing Google Analytics is a huge step toward taking control of your online marketing. It will open your eyes to valuable information about your website visitors and display the data in an easy-to-read, easy-to-understand format. Over time, you will see trends that you could not have discovered any other way.

Retweet Rank

Retweet Rank (see Figure 22-4) is one of many useful free Twitter tools that let you track the number of retweets you're getting compared to other Twitter users. Using it is as easy as entering your Twitter handle in the search box and clicking the Go button. You'll instantly see where you rank in terms of retweet power, and you can scroll down to see your latest and most popular retweets. It's not an exact science, and relies on a relative percentile score, but it does provide an idea of how much your content is being shared.

Twitalyzer

Twitalyzer takes a few unique looks at your popularity and involvement on Twitter. It's not ideal for new users because it relies on metrics drawn from your tweeting history over several months. But even newbies can look at the information it can provide by typing in any

FIGURE 22-4

Retweet Rank provides a useful indicator of how often you're being retweeted.

Twitter handle in the search box. The result shows influence, which is defined by the number of followers you have (relative reach), the number of times you are retweeted (relative authority), the number of times you retweet (relative generosity), the number of times you are referenced by others (relative clout), and the number of updates you publish over a seven-day period (relative velocity).

You can try out Twitalyzer free before choosing one of its monthly subscription options, which costs $4.99 for individual users, $29.99 for business users, and $99.99 for agencies.

TweetStats

TweetStats is best described as colorful graphs of your Twitter life. It renders your tweet timeline as a bar chart and shows all your activity since you started. TweetStats provides a pleasant overview of overall activity, including tweet volume and density plus aggregate daily and hourly tweets. The tweet timeline is particularly useful because it shows your daily average number of tweets. It's a useful tool that you might want to use once every couple of months to check the trends. TweetStats is free but has a Donate option for grateful users.

Influence Measures

Free to use influence measuring tools such as PeerIndex, Klout, and more recently Kred are useful in showing those people you influence the most and, likewise, those who most influence your personal brand. They work on different algorithms and assumptions that are incredibly complex and difficult to understand. The companies don't seem able to explain exactly how they work, putting their accuracy into question. Try them out and make up your own mind!

"Your hopes and friends are infinite."

—*King Henry VIII*

23

Miscellaneous Tools

My final selection of Twitter tools is something of a mixed bag. I have test-driven them all, and each has a place in my toolkit for adding value to my personal brand on Twitter. They range from tools to track who has unfollowed you to tools that help you with your #FF Follow Friday recommendations. All are easy to use and practical. Whether you choose to incorporate all or just a few into your toolkit after trying them out, I guarantee you'll have fun in the process.

ManageFlitter

This useful tool (see Figure 23-1) lets you clean up and manage your followers in just a few clicks. You can find out who is following you back, discover who has been inactive for a long time, and link your Google+ account to your Twitter account. I find the free version of ManageFlitter (limited to 1,000 follows or unfollows a day) is ample for my needs, but you can upgrade to a pro version providing unlimited usage for $12 per month.

Buffer

I find the Buffer app (see Figure 23-2) to be an incredibly useful tool for scheduling my daily personal-brand show's content on Twitter. It's different from the scheduling options in HootSuite and TweetDeck that help you schedule and send your tweets at a particular date and time but that have you enter details like titles and URLs, which can be time-consuming. Buffer has a different approach: You simply drop your links in your Buffer account to have this clever tool queue them for future publishing. Or you can use one of Buffer browser extensions to make adding tweets as simple as clicking an icon.

Buffer also has built-in analytics that let you monitor the impact of your tweets. Click the Analytics button in your Buffer account to see the number of

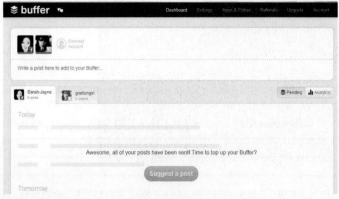

FIGURE 23-1

ManageFlitter is a useful tool for keeping track of those who aren't following you back and those accounts that are inactive.

retweets, number of clickthroughs, and the number of people each tweet you've "buffered" has reached. Buffer even sends you a reminder when you need to top up your scheduled tweets.

Buffer offers three account options. The free version lets you schedule 10 posts per day to Twitter, Facebook, and/or LinkedIn. The pro option costs $10 per month and lets you add up to six social accounts and increases your scheduling allowance to 50 posts a day. The premium version costs $99 per month and offers team scheduling options with unlimited accounts and unlimited posts daily.

FIGURE 23-2

Buffer lets you know when it needs topping up with tweets.

TweetLevel

TweetLevel (see Figure 23-3) is a great tool for checking both Twitter topics and Twitter users. You can also conveniently search and analyze hashtags to find out how popular your hashtags have been and to explore others. You can order Tweets by any results, including influence, popularity, engagement, and trust. TweetLevel also gives you a great array of options to find new people to follow.

Created by @jonnybentwood at the global PR agency Edelman, TweetLevel is free to users on a permanent beta basis, to ensure the continual improvement of its features and functionality.

Twitter Tussle

Twitter Tussle is a totally free, fun, and addictive way to compare keywords on Twitter to see which is the more popular in the Twitterverse; in other words, which is being tweeting about the most. The tool is incredibly simple to use: Just visit the website www.twittertussle.com and enter any two words in the text boxes in the middle of the page. Then just click Tussle and watch the two blue Twitter birds enter the ring and fight it out over the popularity of their respective words.

Although a procrastination app, Twitter Tussle is a great way to compare how your personal brand is faring by measuring the popularity of your keywords and of your Twitter handle itself alongside other competitors in your particular sector.

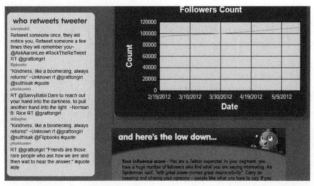

FIGURE 23-3

As well as providing a score based on influence (like Klout and Kred), TweetLevel also look at factors such as trust and can explore the popularity of your hashtags as well as your tweets.

FollowFriday Helper

FollowFriday Helper is an easy-to-use, totally free, and very useful Twitter tool, letting you see exactly who has mentioned you over the past seven days so you can reciprocate with an #FF recommendation or a #ThankYou via the tool itself. As someone who likes to thank all those who share my content as often as possible, this tool has become an invaluable part of my weekly Twitter toolkit, saving me time and ensuring that no-one gets overlooked.

Twitition

If you have a particular cause that you believe strongly in and want to invite others to join, Twitition is the tool for you. With it, you can create all sorts of online petitions for your campaigns and add the support of people around the world using your personal brand's clout to ensure they tweet their allegiance. It's completely free to use, and anyone can generate a campaign in just a few clicks. It's an innovative way of earning money for charities you support or events you are sponsoring.

Blether

Blether lets you easily start a group chat with your followers. There are other tools that you can use to organize private chats such as Zendit and Tribalfish, but Blether offers the simplest option by far, and it's free. Log in to Blether and enter the Twitter handles of the people you want to invite to your chat. Then give your chat a name by typing one into the subject box. The Twitter users you added are sent an invitation to join the chat, and the conversation can be followed in Blether through a simple chat area.

The creator of the chat has the control to remove a user, include more people, or move the chat to another window under a different name. Blether runs on any platform that uses URLs, including computers, smartphones, and tablets.

Nearby Tweets

Nearby Tweets (see Figure 23-4) is a free geolocation Twitter tool for social networking, building customer relationships, and monitoring real-time buzz. The tool is extremely useful for getting to know what's being

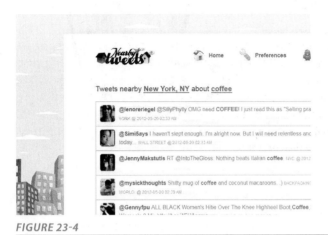

FIGURE 23-4

Nearby Tweets lets you get up-close and personal with those in your neighborhood using Twitter.

tweeted about in a particular location in real time, letting users network and connect with locals, find the tweeters nearby who have similar interests, monitor word of your personal brand in a specific location, or organize a local tweetup.

TweetBeep

Last, but definitely not least in my guide to the best Twitter tools for your personal branding toolkit, is TweetBeep. This incredibly useful tool has been featured in the *Wall Street Journal* and *New York Times* as one to watch. It's like a Google Alerts for Twitter, keeping track of tweets that mention you, your products, your company, and anything that you ask it to track; it provides hourly updates. You can even keep track of who is tweeting your website or blog, even if they use a shortened URL (like those generated by Bit.ly or Tinyurl.com).

TweetBeep is a superior tool for online reputation management, catching all your replies and mentions, finding job and networking opportunities, and keeping up on your favorite interests. The excellent basic version is free to use, providing you don't mind advertisements; for $20 per month, you get 200 ad-free alerts and a 15 minute alert option.

Index